MW01138763

Crazy About Words

To give to Helena

For Ann —
So good to
see you again!

Happy Wording!

Joe Du Cla

Joe McKay's

Crazy
About
Words

... toasting our language since 2003!

The New
Atlantian Library

The New Atlantian Library
is an imprint of
ABSOLUTELY AMAZING eBOOKS

Published by Whiz Bang LLC, 926 Truman Avenue, Key West, Florida 33040, USA

Crazy About Words copyright © 2013 by Joe Mc Kay. Electronic compilation/ print editions copyright © 2013 by Whiz Bang LLC.
Original cover art by Mary Jo Douglas
Photographed by Richard Mizdal

All rights reserved. No part of this book may be reproduced, scanned, or transmitted in any form or by any means, electronic or mechanical, including photocopying, recording, or any information storage and retrieval system, without permission in writing from the publisher. Please do not participate in or encourage piracy of copyrighted materials in violation of the author's rights. Purchase only authorized ebook editions.

While the author has made every effort to provide accurate information at the time of publication, neither the publisher nor the author assumes any responsibility for errors, or for changes that occur after publication. Further, the publisher does not have any control over and does not assume any responsibility for author or third-party websites or their contents.

For information contact:
Publisher@AbsolutelyAmazingEbooks.com

ISBN-13: 978-1494705640
ISBN-10: 1494705648

To my Uncle,
Eugene Mc Caffrey,
who never stopped encouraging me.

Crazy
About
Words

INTRODUCTION

I KNOW THE MATH is there, but I'm still astonished that the 12,000 to 25,000 words average people know today, plus the thousands more in the dictionary, are constructed simply from various combinations of our twenty-six letter alphabet. Some of them are uncanny... consider "quaff" and "coif." Most have interesting histories, and have evolved in meaning, spelling, and/or pronunciation.

And from this vast palette of words, writers have wrung some of the most beautiful lines of poetry and startling sentences of prose imaginable. William Cullen Bryant refers to a good poem as "clothed in words of flame;" and Emerson, speaking as a writer, considered himself "a manufacturer of rockets."

From the time in high school when I first laid eyes on "Beowulf" and then Chaucer's 14th century "Canterbury Tales," I wondered how our English language got from then to now. But it remained, for me, a mostly unstudied phenomenon until 2003. That's when I began to lead discussion groups on words and language in the Lifetime Learning Program in my community. I named my course, and the blog writing I later commenced, **"Crazy About Words."**

And I was hooked! Our incredible English language is full of marvels. They lure me to investigate the breadth and depth of how it all came about, and to share my enthusiasm and discoveries, as I do here in this collection of essays.

We tend, for the most part, to think of the word "evolution" in connection with living organisms, but the evolutionary process is alive and well in anything that experiences change and development, from automobile design to "evolving feelings."

Certainly English has earned the right to be called a "living language." It has evolved remarkably to the point where it is the most sophisticated and flexible language on Earth, adaptable to a change-a-minute world in which it has come to function as the *lingua franca*.

In the decade before Al Gore invented the Internet ☺ Robert Mac Neil, co-author of "The Story of English," had this to say, "Broadcasting has democratized the publication of language, often at its most informal, even undressed. Now the ears of the educated cannot escape the language of the masses. ... Hidden in this is a simple fact: our language is not the special private property of the language police, or grammarians, or teachers, or even great writers. ... English belongs to everybody: the funny turn of phrase that pops into the mind of a farmer telling a story; or the travelling salesman's dirty joke; or the teenager saying, "Gag me with a spoon;" or the pop lyric ... all contribute, are all as valid as the tortured image of the academic, or the line the poet sweats over for a week."

Now, in the age of the Internet, this democratization is even more pronounced. I read recently that, thanks to the proliferation of "slang," aka "non-standard English," over the Internet, there are now 2500 words for "drunk!" I applaud this language trend. It is but one example of people breaking out and being creative, and it is creativity that must fuel each of our endeavors in the future if we are to be fully functioning humans in a global world.

In creating my monthly **"Crazy About Words"** column, I wanted not only to celebrate this trend, but to share our unique English language heritage. I want to contribute to making us all aware of the threads that connect our language to the past and to the billions of non-English speakers with whom we share this planet. As we find ourselves increasingly interdependent, it is helpful, I believe, to realize how much language history we have in common.

And I believe that doing so can be fun, interesting, mentally challenging, and often "WOW!"

This collection includes most of the columns I've written over the past four years, a few autobiographical essays inspired by a word, and a poem or two. I've also cited several of the Websites specializing in words and language that I visit regularly. And I talk about a children's literacy non-profit, The Dictionary Project, which I enthusiastically support.

I sincerely hope you will enjoy these **"Crazy About Words"** essays in the same spirit in which I have written them.

- Joe Mc Kay
October 2013

Opening Words

OPENING A COLUMN on the subject of **"choice opening words"** is a challenge. But there ... it's done.

They **are the welcome mat**. I'll bet no words in any work of fiction are more carefully, and painfully chosen by the author than those the reader first encounters. Sure, the title page, dedication, table of contents, and introduction should invite the reader in. But just watch a browser at a bookstore and you'll *know* where the threshold is.

Hemingway said that when he was having trouble getting a new story going, he realized he was trying too hard, writing too elaborately, and needed to **start with "one true sentence."**

Here's how he opened *The Old Man and The Sea* in 1952: **"He was an old man who fished alone in a skiff in the Gulf Stream and he had gone eighty-four days now without taking a fish."** His use of the word "now" propels us into the scene and the emotion.

Similarly, although a good friend recommended her young daughter-in-law's first novel, I would not likely have read and thoroughly enjoyed it, unless **"It was a small-town June wedding, and the bride was seventy-eight."** had not drawn me in. Neither life nor literature often celebrates the nuptials of people that age, for reasons *Emily Gray Tedrowe* explores so beautifully in *Commuters,* 2010.

I checked out a few novels I've read in the recent past to see how welcoming they seem in retrospect, how clean and true their first words. What do you think?

"I have been here so long that even the sea gulls must recognize me. They must pass the word along about me from generation to generation, from egg to egg."... *I Cover the Waterfront, by Max Miller,* 1932. The whole sentence is inviting, but the clincher for me is "from egg to egg." I don't know how I originally came by this book. I found it in a box in my attic, and read it three times one summer, then found an original copy online with its dustcover still intact ... a treasure!

"The name of the town was Beautyburg. It was one of those ironical tongue-in-cheek names which somehow get themselves attached to Pennsylvania mining towns, part mocking, part hopeful, part comic, part truthful."... *The Long Discovery, by John Burgan,* 1950. It hooked me, (how could anyone resist not wanting to know more about a place called Beautyburg?) and evidently not for the first time. It had been sitting on my shelf unread for years, a garage sale purchase marked "50 cents."

"Laura was my sister, alive those four years before I was born—born not to protect her, although I made the mistake of thinking so, but to witness the show of her survival."... *A History of Silence, by Barbara Neil,* 1998. Laura wasn't simply "four years older than I." I stayed with this gem for the terrific writing style more than anything else.

"Devils," Ahmad thinks. **"These devils seek to take away my God."** ... *Terrorist, by John Updike,* 2006. Delivers bone-chilling suspense; I couldn't put it down.

"I shook his hand for the first time in 1967. I was a second-year student at Columbia then, a know-nothing boy with an appetite for books..." ... *Invisible, by Paul Auster,* 2009. I received a copy for my birthday that year because I am a devoted fan of the author, but finished it in two days because I could relate personally to those opening words.

A friend told me recently that her favorite opening words are, **"Last night I dreamt I went to Manderley again."**... *Rebecca, by Daphne du Maurier,* 1938. Consider how rhythmic that sentence is, mainly because the first four words end in "t" and how much less rhythmic it would read had the author been American and chosen to use "dreamed." Or try and substitute any other place name for the fictional "Manderley." (Chicago definitely doesn't work!) Consider too the power that fictional words have: In 1998, Enya, the Irish musician/singer, bought Victoria Castle, built in 1840 on the Irish coast, and renamed it "Manderley" for *Rebecca,* her favorite novel.

Of course we all have favorite books that took reading the first 100 pages to "really get into." And even some of these begin with memorable opening words like, **"Call me Ishmael."** But that's a story for another day.

Greek Debt

IF EACH OF US English speakers paid back a penny each time we used a **word that originated as a proper name in Greek mythology**, Greece would be solvent in no time. When you say you're headed **east**, you owe **Eos**, the goddess of Dawn. If you wax poetic on the magic of **night**, you're beholden to **Nyx**, the god of Night. You're indebted to **Vulcan**, the god of Fire, when you use the word **volcano.** And when you take your daily **aphrodisiac**, you must thank **Aphrodite,** the goddess of Love.

The Greeks could make a national industry of their rich mythology. And generating new **myths** is something they're pretty good at too. For years, Athenian **plutocrats** succeeded in declaring only **3%** of the actual number of residential swimming pools to the government. Recently, tax collectors used Google Earth satellite photography to prove that there were 180,000 not 6,000 pools subject to property tax. Oops! Science trumps the myth of **Ploutos,** god of Wealth, Greed, and Worldly Goods.

The idea for this column came as I read *Swim...Why We Love the Water,* Lynn Sherr's wonderful brief anthology of swimming lore, written in conjunction with her preparation to swim the Hellespont (now known as the Dardanelles) from Europe to Asia in 2011. She relates the legendary tale of Leander, an ordinary laboring man, who trysted with **Hero,** a virgin priestess of **Aphrodite**, by swimming the Hellespont each night and back the next morning. One night a storm doused Hero's lamp; Leander lost his way and drowned. Overwhelmed with grief, Hero jumped from her tower to join him in the afterlife, and lent her name forever to those who perform **heroic** acts. Let's not forget that the first **hero** was female!

The myths galore that comprise "Greek **Mythology**" were stories made up to relate the unknown to the known, to explain natural phenomena, and to guide moral behavior. Most of these stories centered around gods and those closest to them.

When you talk about the **hyacinths** in your garden, you are indebted to **Hyacinthus**, the handsome youth loved by the god **Apollo**, who accidentally kills him with a discus, and in whose memory Apollo grows a new flower.

For his role in the unsuccessful revolt of the **Titans** against the **Olympians, Atlas** was condemned by **Zeus** to stand at the edge of **Gaia...the Earth,** and carry the heavens on his shoulders, to prevent them from re-entering their primordial embrace with earth. For his forbearance, **Atlas** got to give his name to the **top vertebra of the spine**, the point where the weight was concentrated. Later, the myth got confused; Atlas was depicted bearing the weight of Earth on his shoulders, and his name lent to **a compilation of terrestrial maps**. (The bronze Atlas sculpture at Rockefeller Center in NYC has it right, depicting celestial spheres, not a solid orb.) Angelo Siciliano (1892-1972) reinvented himself in 1929 as bodybuilder, **Charles Atlas,** whose strength evoked that of the original Atlas. His memorable ad, "Give me 15 minutes a day, and I'll give you a new body," was one of the longest running of all time. He is the god of Skinny Men who want to look more muscular.

The story of **Tantalus** is that of another son of a god, condemned to stand knee-deep in water in **Hades**, for betraying the trust of the gods at the dinner table. When he bends down to drink, the water recedes, and when he reaches up for fruit from the tree above him, it is just beyond his grasp. Every time we say **tantalizing**, we owe a penny!

My personal favorite is "the weaver's tale," the story of **Arachne**, a maiden who was transformed into a spider by **Athena**, the goddess of the Arts, for challenging her to a weaving contest. That was a major no-no, another Eve Harrington gone awry, for which she earned a permanent place in **entomology** as an **arachnid**. And this is the point where **entomology,** the study of insects, meets **etymology,** the study of the origin of words.

With plots like **Dostoyevsky's *Crime and Punishment***, a cast of characters longer than forty years' worth of *All My Children*, and with such incredible **logogenesis...word creation**, Greek Mythology is well worth exploiting for fun and profit.

Oh, To Be a Sandwich!
...or...
What Does It Take to
Become an Eponym?

IF YOU WERE BORN in **July** or **August** by **Caesarean** section, you have an **eponymous** connection... the first and last names of an early Roman Emperor, **Julius or Augustus Caesar.**

But, do you ever wish you could *be* an **eponym**, with **something named after you**...something more enduring than your not-totally-reliable progeny?

John Montagu, 4th Earl of **Sandwich**, James Brudnell, 7th Earl of **Cardigan,** and, no kidding, Joao **Marmalado** (1450-1510) of Portugal, are all folks whose names were taken by the items they originated, which survive centuries later.

Eponyms also attribute to something discovered, like **America** (although Amerigo Vespucci must give indigenous people their due!), something invented, like the **derringer** (Henry Derringer, American gunsmith), or something inspired, like the **axel** (Axel Paulsen, Norwegian figure skater). They surprise us frequently... we just never think that there might have been a **Mr.**

Doyley, a 17ᵗʰ century London draper, who inspires the tatting of **doilies** to this day!

It is fitting that **sideburns** are named for **Ambrose Burnside**, Union Army General, Governor, and Rhode Island Senator. Google a picture of him and see sideburns run amok! They are not a beard because he left his chinny-chin-chin clean-shaven, for a style affected uniquely by him. Originally called **burnsides,** the syllables were later inverted.

Some eponyms are very subtle, like **maudlin,** which derives from Mary **Magdalene**'s effusive sentimental behavior in the New Testament. Others are more obvious, like **ritzy** after Caesar Ritz, Swiss hotelier. Don Quixote's tilting against windmills is forever preserved in the idealistic **quixotic.**

Eponyms are derived not only from people's names, but from the **names of places**, real or fictional, like **serendipity**. It comes from the Persian fairy tale, "The Three Princes of Serendip" (an old name for Sri Lanka), in which the heroes "were always making discoveries, by accidents and sagacity, of things they were not in quest of." It is regarded as one of the ten English words most difficult to translate precisely.

The **mazurka,** a dance from Mazury, is named for a region of Poland, and **madras,** that wonderful cotton fabric, from a city now renamed Chennia, the 5ᵗʰ most populous in India. (Back in "the day" I had to have **bleeding madras**, whose dyes were not fast, so that it looked different every time it was washed...cool!)

Writing this column, I have to be careful of something not so cool, **malapropism,** after the fictional character,

Mrs. Malaprop from Sheridan's "Rivals." She was noted for her blunders in the use of words.

Two of my personal favorite eponyms come from nineteenth century circus performers, who died before their time only fifteen years apart.

Jumbo, whose name is from a Swahili word *jumbe* meaning "chief," was a 6½ ton French Sudanese elephant, born in 1861. He toured the US and Canada with "The Greatest Show on Earth," the Barnum & Bailey Circus, where he was the largest of its 30 elephants, a big hit with the public, and featured on most of the Circus' posters. On the night of 9/15/1885, he was hit and killed by an express freight train in St. Thomas, Ontario. The resulting publicity inspired "**Jumbo-size**" food items like hot dogs and sausages. The word stuck to describe anything large or huge, including Boeing's Jumbo Jets.

Jules **Leotard** (1842-1870) invented the flying trapeze and popularized the one-piece gymwear that bears his name. He joined the *Cirque Napoleon*, went on to international stardom, and inspired the 1867 hit song "The Daring Young Man on the Flying Trapeze." Although he sprained his ankle in a bad fall in Boston, he died in Spain of smallpox.

So now you have some idea of what it takes to achieve **eponymous** status. Remember... that favorite lunch food, the ham **sandwich** could just as easily have been called a ham **sullivan,** or a ham **smith.**

If your name is **John,** you don't have to bother...you're already a famous necessity.

Poor Little Orphans

IT'S A SURE SIGN you're crazy ... about words, at least, when you come to think of them as people. I began to realize this about myself some time back as I was checking out the etymology of **bamboozled**. I was surprised that it was as old as 1703, but floored when I saw that it was categorized as **"origin unknown."** How could etymologists not know how such a **nifty** word originated?

Sometime later, I saw that **bludgeon (1868)** was in that same category, then **flirt (1877)** and **punk (1596)**. I wrote them down on a sheet of paper and printed **"origin unknown"** at the top. I felt like a character in a Dickens novel, a benevolent one, gathering in orphans from the street. Now, every time I come across a word with that label, or **"origin uncertain,"** I feel parental and add it to my list.

Most words are like children whose roots can be traced as pedigrees are ... **axiomatic** from Greek, **obsequious** from Latin, **maladroit** from French, **galore** from Irish Gaelic, or **assassin** from Arabic, to list a few. They come to us from long lines of traceable language.

Or they are new words, easily traceable in this Google era, e.g., **app** (short for application and the 2010 "word of the year"), **tweet** (a 2009 winner which defines a message containing no more than 140 characters and delivered by Twitter), and **locavore** (a person who eats only food grown and produced within a certain number of miles of his home). No etymologist of the future, with the prowess of the Internet at his fingertips, will fail to detect the precise origin of words like these.

Actually, the more I get to know of etymologists' exacting work, the more I appreciate what they *have* been able to trace with certainty. E.g., **genro** (a group of elder Japanese statesmen, formerly advisers to the emperor) originated as two words in Ancient Mandarin. I am in awe of the lexicological digging involved here; it's akin to archeology.

Here are a few surprises that defied etymologists in the first two-thirds of the twentieth century and remain on the **"origin unknown" list**: -**chad** ("a bit of paper punched out from a data card." It became world famous in the 2000 US presidential election; it's been traced to 1947, but how did the word come about? ... *perhaps* from the Scots "gravel," is the best they can do; -**copacetic** ("very satisfactory," 1919... a fun word; I expected it to be of Greek origin); -**gimmick** ("an ingenious or novel mechanical device, gadget," 1926... you could have a fun time with fellow word lovers inventing an etymology for it!) They each have a special place in my heart.

Another favorite is **quaff (1529)** thought perhaps to be imitative. I've tried, even wiped my lips with the back of my hand, but quaff after quaff, I can't get myself to sound like the word.

Simoleon (1895-1900) is a cool slang word for a dollar. How I wish we knew its origins. It's bound to be interesting.

At the top of my list is **acne**. While not exactly of unknown origin, it had a peculiar beginning, in that it was the result of a manuscript error, aka "typo." "Acme" was the intended word, after "the head of a pimple" : (... but "acne" stuck (and most of us were stuck with it at some point in our young lives!). So it's fitting that the last word in my alphabetical list of "origins unknown," **zit,** originated in 1966, the last year that etymologists could not detect a word's origin. Since then, the huge computer databases available make it virtually impossible for a word to be born without a birth certificate. It marks the end of an etymological era.

Confetti

MY LIFE IS STREWN with bits of paper, words scribbled on them, and shards of newspapers and magazines with words or phrases circled. I find them in my pockets, all over the house, serving as bookmarks, on dry cleaning tickets I now can't surrender, on cash register receipts, and restaurant napkins. I seldom remember to carry one of the little pads purchased to keep words I hear or read organized in one place.

I'm sitting with a small pile of these jots I've gathered to share. They look like large **confetti**. So let's do a gala!

On the day of "the wedding," **"regalia"** was used all day long to describe the royals' dress (except for Princess Beatrice's hat! That was called many other things.) The word originally applied to the *symbols* of royalty, e.g., the **crown & scepter;** gradually, to the **symbols of rank**, like military officers' brass; and, eventually, to **any finery in dress.** It's a Latin plural (as is **confetti**) used as a singular noun in English to describe, sometimes facetiously, **any dressed-up look.** Used in this sense, the **opposite/antonym** of **"regalia"** that I like best is **"rags."**

I came across **"spavined"** in Morris West's 1963 novel, "The Shoes of the Fisherman:" "He had flung his cap at the whirling windmills, but when the time came to assault them...how would he be then? A knight in shining armor...Or an aging Quixote on a **spavined** nag, an object of laughter for men and angels?"

For hundreds of years, it's been used only to refer to a **bony-hipped** horse. But why not broaden its definition a bit and extend its use? Aren't there millions of humans in the world who would rather think of themselves as "spavined" than "arthritic?" It sounds more elegant, begs elaboration, and might just save the word from becoming archaic.

David Brooks is helping coin a couple of neologisms. In his latest book, "The Social Animal," he writes of **"sanctimommies"/ mothers who critique their peers' parenting skills** and **"extracurricular sluts"/ whose kids participate in too many organized after-school activities.** No one has more fun with our language than he.

The hero of a 2005 novel, "Indecision," by Benjamin Kunkel is described as "the 21st-century literary descendant of Holden Caulfield" except that he suffers from **"abulia," a disease characterized by a lack of will or initiative.** "Dwight knows that his **indecisiveness** makes him a sociological cliché."

"Fracking" is the buzzword in the world of energy technology. It describes a new, economical method of hydraulic fracturing of underground shale rock allowing vast supplies of otherwise trapped natural gas to flow. Promoters say it's a safe method to tap into 100-plus years' supply in the US & Canada; detractors say it may pose a threat to drinking water. It's controversial, and **"fracking"** will soon be on everyone's lips....a new "f-word" at last!

One syndicated version of **cryptograms** is called "Cryptoquote." I love to work these puzzles and watch the wise words of well-known people emerge from the eyesore of encryption. A recent cryptoquote yielded this from Dr. Seuss: "... There is no one alive who is **youer** than you." It's a psychological principle, a spiritual concept, and a great word all rolled into one! Seuss could have properly used "more you," but, oh, how I appreciate his lexi-play that, at last, gives us a homonym of "ewer."

I hope you will accumulate some confetti of your own and enjoy a party with fellow word lovers.

Remembering a Special Word

THERE IT WAS, spelled out in all its glory...
O-C-H-S-E-N-S-C-H-W-A-N-N-Z-S-U-P-P-E. I'd never seen a word like it.

At the end of my first day in West Germany, I had changed into civvies and walked off base from Coleman Barracks, outside Mannheim, to a modest country **gasthaus (literally, guest house, a small bar and restaurant)** at the end of a farm lane, just a few yards from the Rhine River.

From its position at the head of the menu and its final five letters, I figured OCHSENSCHWANNZSUPPE must be soup. But what kind? ... I had no idea. When the waiter came to take my order, I wanted the word. I pointed to its 19 letters, spread out like a banner at the top of the left inside page of the **speisencarte...menu.**

"Ja, ochsenschwannzsuppe?" he asked, pronouncing all five beautiful syllables slowly and clearly. I loved hearing the word; it was so exotic. It occurred to me that the only German words I knew for sure at that point were **gesundheit** and **marzipan** (originally Italian, meaning "march bread").

"Ja" I replied, taking to the language with lust, "ochsenschwannzsuppe."

I had made my first transaction in a foreign language, although my pronunciation was risible.

The waiter seemed pleased, all affability, as though it were a triumph of understanding for both of us. Then, as so often occurs when only one of two speakers is native to a language, he was encouraged to go on and speak a few sentences, quickly, and replete with the gutturals I would come to love. I only understood, from the uptick in his voice, he had ended with a question.

I decided to just say "Ja." I've always been a culinary adventurer, able to eat anything, so it didn't matter much to me what I had ordered. I could wait to find out.

But I hadn't been able to wait to get out among the German people, to experience "exotic" after 23 years during which I'd never traveled further from my native New York City than Columbus, Ohio.

The **ochsenschwannzsuppe** arrived, hardy and incongruous on that warm summer day, a thick, dark brown concoction with bits of meat, more like gravy than soup, and incredibly delicious. What I had agreed to with my second "Ja" was a huge platter of varied, healthy-looking **brotchen... rolls** with pads of butter stacked neatly at one end, slices of golden cheese at the other, and a smaller plate with pickled beets, cauliflower, and onions. I gauged it was enough, no multiplying miracle necessary, to feed my whole platoon. And all of it, it turned out, was provided at no extra charge.

I walked out to that gasthaus many times during my two-year tour of duty, and was always greeted with a big smile and a welcoming, **"ochsenschwannzsuppe?"** Before I returned to the States, I asked the waiter/owner for that menu because the word held such a special place in my life. It had prompted me to study German and I became quite fluent.

This memory came back recently as I was preparing a session on compound words for a "Crazy About Words" class I originated and teach in my community. I love the fact that languages stretch and adapt, through compounding, to express new concepts. I read that other Germanic languages compound by stringing out a single word endlessly, e.g., **eriebnisgastronomisches ... theme restaurant**, while we English speakers use open compounds like "oxtail soup."

I think my love of compound words was born the day I first saw **ochsenschwannzsuppe** and I thank all the oxen that have donated their tails to making this word so memorable.

March and Other Ambiguities

WHAT WITH "in like a lamb, out like a lion, and vice versa," and "beware the ides of March" hovering over us, March is an **iffy** month.

"Well, old hag, the ides have come," mocked Julius Caesar to the seer on his way to the Senate on 3/15/44 b.c. "Ah, yes, but they have not gone," she retorted ambiguously, a short while before he was stabbed 23 times by a *coalition* of his **iffy** friends.

I really wanted to use **"iffy"** in writing. It's such a wonderful creation...an **adjective coaxed out of a conjunction by the simple addition of the underappreciated little suffix, -y**. Like the currently controversial "truthy," it leaves me feeling **uncertain** every time I hear it, exactly as intended by whoever first used it, I suppose.

But the dictionary labels it a **colloquialism,** meaning it originated in informal conversation, and is "not suitable for formal speech or writing," such as you're experiencing right here! Ah, how different things might be had Dickens written, "They were very **iffy** times." in opening "A Tale of Two Cities!"

In keeping with the **"iffiness"** that abounds this month, let's look at a few words, phrases, and facts I've come across recently that demonstrate, in one way or another, just how **ambiguous (from Latin, ambigere, to wander about)** life is.

I like the word **amphiboly (an ambiguous grammatical structure in a sentence)** and these nice examples of it: Disraeli once said to a man who handed him his book to read, "I shall waste no time reading it." And how about a recent news story headlined, "Victims Advocate Counts Yellowstone Wolves." (say whaaat?), or the made-for-Groucho road sign, "Eat Here and Get Gas."

Humpty Dumpty got Alice going when he said, "When I use a word, it means just what I choose it to mean – nothing more nor less." To which she replied, "The question is whether you can make words mean so many different things." (It's a fact, according to the OED, that the 500 most used English words have an average of 23 different meanings! The word "round," for example, has 70 distinct definitions. That explains much of the ambiguity in our beautiful language.)

Legerdemain (pronounced 'lejerdeman') is a neat word, meaning **sleight of hand.** Sy Safransky in an interview about *The Sun,* said, "...as if I were a magician and my ad-free, nonprofit magazine an elaborate feat of **legerdemain,** each issue another rabbit pulled from my hat..."

Lagniappe, (pronounced 'lanyap') per the dictionary, comes from Creole meaning **a trifling present given to customers by a salesman.** (In the Gulf Coast region of the US, it is used popularly to mean **a little something extra.**) The **iffy** thing about its stated origin is it doesn't sound like either a French or Spanish root. Sure enough, further research indicates that its origin is likely a

Quechua word, **nyapa,** that made its way into Spanish, then traveled up from the Inca empire into New Orleans where the French article, **la**, was added. Ayelet Waldman, author of the recent best seller, "Bad Mother," rewarded readers who preordered her book with a copy of one by her famous husband, Michael Chabon, "as a **lagniappe,**" according to the Wall Street Journal. The couple reside in New Orleans. (And I'd call that a "big" something extra! He's one of my favorite contemporary authors.)

As this **iffy** month barrels past the ides, the time of the **equinox (half night-**half day), will be upon us. We might look on that as another example of March indecisiveness. But no ifs, ands, or buts about it, the longer days say that Spring will be here at last. And whether March goes out like a lion or a lamb, the weather is going to get better... **maybe!**

Katherine Hepburn said of Humphrey Bogart, "He walked straight down the center of the road. **No maybes.** Yes or no." So, Bogie is an antidote to March **iffiness**!

Guide Words

IT STILL IMPRESSES ME that the 100,000 plus words in my dictionary (2006 pages in the American Heritage, 4th Edition) are each constructed simply from some combination of letters derived from our 26-letter alphabet. From **aardvark** to **zyzzyva,** we have managed to create the most expressive language imaginable, the toolbox of writers, poets, and all who use and appreciate words.

The beginning of a new year puts many of us in a reflective mood. As that mood extends to my writing this column, I wonder what single word I might select as my **"guide word for the new year."** Looking at a smorgasbord of candidates, I quickly realize that I have long regarded **"attitude"** as basic to just about everything in life.

It's a great word that originally had a **physical** meaning, the **"position of something relative to some other physical thing"** (e.g., an aircraft or a ballet dancer assumes an attitude). It was later adopted by our ancestor-wordsmiths looking for a word to describe a **"mental or emotional position relative to some aspect of life"** (e.g., a person has a positive or negative attitude about money).

Because we all have the power to wake up each day and assume the **attitude** we choose, and so set the course for "the first day of the rest of our lives," I rank it **my #1 word**.

Viktor Frankl, Dachau survivor, when asked upon liberation in 1945 to describe his experience, simply said, "I learned a lot about myself in these past three years." In his book, "Man's Search for Meaning," he says that **"the ultimate human freedom is to choose one's attitude."**

Looking at the word again, and noticing that it begins with "a," the **abecedarian** in me comes out, and I reach for a "b" and a "c" word that will fit into this New Year's reflection.

Bittersweet is a nice compound word with a yin and yang quality to it. The strong, fast-growing bittersweet vine chokes its host bushes and trees in growing season, but decorates their bare branches in winter with its glowing red berries encased in orange. Look up on a sunny day in the winter woods, or gather pieces of the vine to bring indoors, and you'll appreciate the -**sweet** end of this word.

Frankl's point was that many life experiences, even the toughest, are **bittersweet,** but we can learn and grow as human beings from each of them if we have **an attitude of openness** and an interest in learning about ourselves relative to Life.

Circumstances, a Latin word meaning, **the things that surround us,** need not dictate our attitude. **Attitude** comes from within us, is self-determined. Imagine you have only six pennies. Are you poor? **Circumstances** might say so. But you give two away with generosity in your heart, then buy a piece of bread with a third, consciously savoring the taste of it. You are rich.

Not a bad **abecedarian** set of words to guide us: **attitude, bittersweet, circumstances.**

Cheers! Here's to a rich and rewarding new year.

Welcome to the "Crazy About Words" Café

...catering to epicurious food & language lovers!

MORE NEW WORDS AND USAGES have evolved around food recently than just about anything else but communications technology. **Foodies** are **grazing** throughout the day, eating many small meals, rather than the old fashioned **three squares (named for a square wooden board on which food was served at inns and from which 'room and board' was derived).**

Tapas... small Spanish savory dishes, typically served with drinks at a bar... is in, and **locavores** are priding themselves on eating nothing that's grown or raised beyond an ever-shorter radius of their homes. **CSAs (Community Supported Agriculture)** are popping up all over, and **cow shares (you get the front quarter; I get the hind)** are burgeoning. People are **tweeting** about it all and e-mailing photos of their food as they eat!

So we're going to visit the "Crazy Café" and sample a few food words, some old... others new, to chew on.

A new reader reminded me, in response to my **"Silent Knights"** column, that **knish** has the distinction of being the only **kn-** word in the dictionary in which **the *k* is pronounced.** It's a Yiddish import from Russia (1916). Think of it as a big Jewish ravioli.

A good friend and successful cookbook author suggested that **barbecue** has an interesting etymology. Indeed, it derives ultimately from ***barabicu***, a Caribe Indian word meaning **sacred fire pit,** and has become a kind of suburban altar. It's also morphed into a sacred symbol, **BBQ.**

Cauliflower too, my friend thought. It's from the Latin ***caulis* (cabbage)** and **flower. It's a standout in a botanical family whose siblings are all edible leafy greens: kale, Brussels sprouts, cabbage and broccoli.**

Looking at the two words together in his e-mail, I was inspired to **barbecue some cauliflower.** Voila! it was some **degustation (tasting or savoring).** If you'd like to **"eat my words,"** steam a trimmed cauliflower head **al denté**, cool and separate the "flowers," toss with a light Tuscan herb or ginger sauce, marinate a few hours, & grill for 10 minutes. Here on Eastern Long Island, home of the LI Cauliflower Association, it might become a **locavore's dream... "Crazy Cauliflower."**

Are you aware of the **cupcake** craze? After losing out some years ago in popularity to muffins and doughnuts, they have roared back in the last few. I read of cupcake parties and cupcake wars, (with decorations like 5-star generals). They are the original **patty cake** of nursery rhyme fame, (**patty cake, patty cake, baker's man,**

bake me a cake as quick as you can) dating to 1796, baked in cups, and designed to serve one person. They are also less rich and heavy than their uncle, **pound cake,** for which the ingredients of both, butter and sugar, were measured by weight (pound) rather than by volume (cup).

And did you know that Carry Nation, the six-foot tall Prohibitionist, also railed against **foreign food**? Clearly she did not win her uphill battle. The first volley sounded when Thomas Jefferson served **"potatoes in the French manner"** at the White House in 1802. Silly Carry, what was she thinking? Where would we be without our beloved **French fries**? ... without being able to hear ourselves say **pommes frites** to a waiter although we speak no French?

Food has, as always, brought us together—for sustenance as well as for good conversation. Happy degustation!

Using 4-letter Words

THE PHRASE, **"four-letter words"** has become almost synonymous with so-called "dirty" words. We're going to change that trend right here, right now, by discussing **a few of my favorites.**

Amok is a fun-to-say word. I overuse it to describe anything "messy and scattered." Technically, it should be reserved to describe the result of a **murderous frenzy,** but I wouldn't get to use it as often as I'm **wont** if I had such reservation. It's a rare import from **Malay, amoq.**

Wont/habit is another I like because I have to consciously round my mouth so it doesn't sound like "want," but not so much that it sounds like "won't."

Acai (ah-sigh-EE) is the new "global super fruit" exported from the Amazon since 2000 in response to "the anti-oxidant craze and rain-forest chic," according to the NYT. It's **the high-energy fruit of a species of palm tree** (coconuts are from another) and a long time staple of the Brazilian diet, getting more expensive for the locals as worldwide demand increases. Look for it at your smoothie shop or cosmetics counter. It's a high-energy word too: has both a **cedilla** under the "c" making it sound like "s" *and* an accent on the "i" emphasizing the "eee" sound.

A **cedilla** (say-dee-ya) shows up in English in the imported word, **"façade."** A word with a cedilla always turns me on, but I *really* go nuts over an **umlaut,** those two little dots used over "a, o, and u" in adopted German words, and pronounced with pursed lips. **Uber** is a perfect umlaut-word, currently very fashionable in English, to mean **very, very/over the top.** The expression, **uber chic** (oober sheek) is a terrific four-letter word meeting of German and French in English. It could only happen in our glorious language!

I like the 4-letter word **doff** (dahff) because it tickles me that it and its **antonym partner, don,** are contracted forms of **"do off"** and **"do on"** but somehow escaped ending up as **"d'off"** and **"d'on".** They are used mostly with clothing items. I remember how men used to **doff,** or **lift their hats,** as they greeted someone with a "How do you do?" Now, I think **doff** every time I see a man in a restaurant wearing a cap. I want to scream, "**doff it.**"

Words ending in "j" are uncommon, so **hadj,** meaning **religious pilgrimage,** especially of a Muslim to Mecca, jumps onto my list. Since 9/11, as we learn more about Muslim culture, we are becoming familiar with many more Arabic words, e.g., **jihad.**

Four-letter words beginning with "i" are relatively few; my short list includes **idyl, imam, impi, iwis** and **iglu.** But **iris** is my favorite as **Iris** was the Greek Goddess of the Rainbow. It's no wonder our eyes, and that wonderful genus of Spring flowers with its variety of colors, took her name.

And finally, my **"f" word** ... I like **fret.** In addition to its most common meaning as a verb for **to worry,** it has distinct noun definitions in architecture and in music. It is a good representative of **polysemous** words, i.e., those **having more than one meaning.**

I could go on and on. But why don't you pick up where I've left off? Go through a letter's worth of pages in the dictionary, and notice a few four-letter words that strike you as those mentioned here do me. Better yet, get hold of the **Scrabble Dictionary** which categorizes all words by length. You'll be amazed at how many interesting **four-letter words** you've *never* heard.

Endangering Species by 'Lexicide'

A FRIEND OF MINE who works at the Cornell University Laboratory of Ornithology in Ithaca, NY, took me on a tour recently while I was visiting my alma mater. At one point she said, "Blue heron chicks are known for committing **siblicide**." I understood immediately that she meant "the stronger siblings kill off the weaker," although, as I verified later, the word is not in the dictionary.

A nice example, I thought, of how when you have a good, sturdy *suffix* like *-cide,* which we all understand, you can add almost anything you like in front of it that you'd like to kill off. It's used with the verb, "commit," when killing our own species as in *suicide, genocide, homocide, infantacide, matricide,* etc. But when we're killing other living things, like plants and bugs, we "use" or "apply" rather than "commit" *herbicide, pesticide, or insecticide* ... which clearly makes it seem less of a crime. How it would alter the justice system if we "committed insecticide!"

At a talk recently, I asked a group to be creative with **making up words** that meant killing something (*-cide* is from the Latin "caedere, to kill"). I got *floracide, faunacide,& sistercide,* and then a gem, "By December 24th. every year, I'm ready to commit **Santacide!**"

Of course, every "-cide" ending is not this suffix, e.g., *decide*. (Although if we added a little "*i*" in there we'd have **deicide** meaning " killing a god.")

Look up suffixes when you notice them; along with *prefixes,* they're called *combination forms* in the dictionary and have an etymology just as words do. Scrabble players aren't allowed to use them unless they also happen to be stand-alone words, like *–able & -ate,* in which case they present a great opportunity to build seven-letter specials like *lovable* and *khanate (the Aga's domain).*

November is the month when my "Crazy About Words" volunteers (participants in my Lifetime Learning class at Peconic Landing, an Adult Community on Long Island) go out to nine local schools to distribute personalized dictionaries to over 300 third-graders. We act as local sponsors on eastern Long Island of **"The Dictionary Project,"** a non-profit organization, to which we donate the cost of copies of "A Student's Dictionary." The book bears a cover photo of planet Earth and the quote, **"The limits of your language are the limits of your world."**

That Ludwig Wittgenstein quote seemed particularly apt when I read in a *National Wildlife* article, **"When Words Become Endangered,"** that the revised edition of the "Oxford Junior Dictionary" has removed numerous nature terms like *wren, dandelion, otter, acorn and beaver*, but has added techie terms like "blog" and "MP3 player." (As we know, the frequency of usage is what gets words edited in and out of dictionaries.)

This "growing disconnect between children and the natural world" is very much the target of my Cornell friend's current project to improve awareness of avian life among urban school children. From my perspective on the importance of words, it's a very worthy endeavor. We cannot commit ***lexicide*** of this sort and expect to maintain a healthy diversity of species on our planet.

Play "Compound Madness"

WHAT'S IN *your* **hibernaculum... location chosen for hibernation,** when you prepare for a rainy day or a long, dark winter?

You might consider wrapping yourself in a simple word game to help pass the time. I like what I call **"Compound Madness."** All that's needed is a pencil, paper, and, of course, your dictionary for when you need to cheat.

Start with any **compound word**, i.e., one that is made up of two separate words, like "inroad." Take the second part of the word, "road" in this case, and make it the first part of another, like "roadside." Then use "side" for the next link... "sideshow" perhaps ... then maybe "show time" (yes, you can use two-word **compound phrases** and **hyphenated words** as well.) Next, "timepiece" comes to mind, then "piecemeal," and so on until you can't get any further, or you emerge from your **hibernaculum!**

The objective is to get as long a chain of compound words and phrases as quickly as possible. When you hit the wall, turn to the dictionary and see if there is a word or phrase you might use to go on ... or, go back a step and see if there is an alternative compound you could have used that will give you further opportunity to continue your chain.

After you've practiced playing it solitaire-fashion for a while, you might like a bit of competition ... a friend who will be a happy loser until he or she gets the hang of **"Compound Madness."** Pencil and paper are not required; you can just alternate until one of you loses the round, and the winner scores a point. Impose a time limit, about 10 or 15 seconds, for each player's turn.

In the course of a good volley, your friend, now up to speed, might serve you "March hare" and you can't return it because you always thought it was "hair lip" (although it didn't make sense) rather than **"hare lip"** after the look of a rabbit's cleft lip, and you never heard of **"hare bell,"** the flower, so you lose the round.

In another instance, after going at it for almost three minutes, back & forth, back & forth, you've served "pot luck" and he came back in 5 seconds with "luck o' the Irish." You're tempted to challenge because **that's really stretching a compound phrase, but you don't want the mad run to end**, and in 1.5 seconds you blurt "Irish coffee" ... so the fun goes on!

In yet another round, you're served "roast pig;" you see an opportunity for a **slam dunk**: rather than return "pigtail" which gives your former friend the chance to come back with "tail pipe" or one of the other 15 tail-compounds listed in my dictionary, you hit him with **"pigsty."**

"Overwhelm" is another good slam dunk ... I only discovered the thirteenth century word, **whelm... engulf, submerge, or bury** recently, thanks to a friend with whom I was playing. You might be inclined to think that **stargaze** would make a slam dunk, but your opponent might be aware that a **gazehound** is **a dog that hunts by sight rather than by scent.** If you challenged her, you learned something new!

Here are a few fun **variations**: play with four people, play over cocktails, make up your own games like "how many links between **upward** and **downward**?" A. three: **ward off, off put, put down.**

Enjoy your **hibernation,** or any time you feel like exercising your brain, with **"Compound Madness."**

How "Honour" Was Lost & "Ain't" Gained Ground ... In the Dictionary Wars

I FELT A SHIVER, a **frisson** of fellowship, when I read this revelation from Emily Dickinson's biographer, "The dictionary was no mere reference book to her; she read it, like a priest his breviary --- over and over, page by page, with utter absorption."

How could she *not* have been smitten by a book so full of itself?

She owned Noah Webster's first *American Dictionary of the English Language* that he had completed in 1828 at the age of 70. Expanded in 1841, it contained 85,000 words. "Honour" was not one of them!

Fifty years after the Revolutionary War, as Americans were still struggling to define their own national identity, Webster booted the English spellings of words like "honour," "programme," and "centre," embraced terms from the Arts & Sciences (gasp!) rather than just literary references, and advocated our use of "a federal language." Infuriated cultural conservatives criticized him for being too inclusive, said his book "bordered on vulgar."

Were he alive today, he might say *his* dictionary is "as American as apple pie." Indeed, "Webster's Third"

(*Webster's Third New International Dictionary of The English Language, Unabridged)*, published in 1961, was so inclusive and descriptive of common usage that it even allowed the long-disdained "ain't" ... "though disapproved by many, and more common in less educated speech, (it is) used orally in most parts of the US by many cultivated speakers esp. in the phrase, "ain't I." Sounds fair enough, eh?

But there has never been a lull in the Dictionary Wars. The publishers of *American Heritage* magazine, after failing to buy out Webster's to halt its sales, geared up and came out with *their* first dictionary in 1969. It favored the prescriptive tradition, guarding what, to their team of lexicographers, is "proper" English.

What would Emily Dickinson say? A line of her own might provide a clue, "A word is dead when it is said, some say/ I say it just begins to live that day."

I am lucky enough to witness words begin to live in the minds of hundreds of children every year at this time. "Crazy About Words" is a local sponsor of "The Dictionary Project"* here on Eastern Long Island. Volunteers personalize and present over 300 copies of "A Student's Dictionary" to Third Graders at eight local schools. I give a short introductory lesson in how to use their dictionary, by first asking the teachers to help **the kids adopt a pet letter** in advance of our school visit.

After volunteers call them up one-by-one to receive their very own first dictionary, I ask the children to turn to the page where words with their "pet letter" begin, and suggest that by the end of the school year they might be experts on words beginning with that letter. Then I ask them each to find a 5-letter word they don't know. On one recent visit, a "C" boy, beaming with the light of discovery, identified **cache.** The boy spelled the word, heard the correct pronunciation (not **catchy!**), and read the definition. Many of the kids, now bristling with recognition of the idea, had anecdotes about **caches** they've known.

I like to think they *will* have an abiding affection for the words they discover on this day.

The inspirational cover of their new dictionary bears a photo of Planet Earth from space and a quote from the Viennese Philosopher, Ludwig Wittgenstein, "The limits of your language are the limits of your world." We close our lesson with a discussion of its meaning.

The Dictionary Project's slogan, "A Dictionary is a Necessity" rings true for me constantly. I look at one of my several grownup's dictionaries and I ask myself, "Where else but in a Dictionary could I find the words, **"brumal,"** **"kyphosis,"** and **"okapi"** between two covers?" ... three words I discovered in my reading this past month and was delighted to squirrel away in my **cache of ken**.

And only with an adult's understanding of the multiple definitions of so many words could I know that **"a Caesarean Section"** might also be **"a neighborhood in Rome"** (from my cache of puns!)

*For more information about "The Dictionary Project," a non-profit organization dedicated to getting every Third Grader his/her own dictionary, and to learn how you might help, go to: "www.dictionaryproject.org"

"Clang-clang-clang went the trolley..."

I RECEIVE MANY requests that sound something like this: "Why don't you do a column on...what do you call it? ... **the kind of word that sounds like what it is... like 'boom' or 'hiss' or 'tinkle.'**" Few of us dare try to spell it (it has eight vowels!) and many of us avoid saying it for fear of tongue-tying ourselves. Dictionary entries usually call it **"imitative."** But most of us seem to sense a language arc connecting us to our primitive past when we get onto the subject of **onomatopoeia.**

Onomatopoeia comes from two Greek words meaning **"name"** and **"I make."** We all hear kids, before they can speak, imitating sounds like **"bow-wow" and "choo-choo."** Parents often use these sound-words in teaching children, who may continue using them long after they learn **dog and train**. Indeed, what honest-with-himself adult doesn't love to join with a group in singing "Old Mac Donald?"

It's no wonder that an early leading theory of the origin of language, formulated by Charles Darwin, has our ancestral grunts imitating the sounds they heard in nature aided by gestures. When they gleefully reproduced those sounds with their lips, larynx, tongues, and breath, they began to experiment, perhaps commanding the cave-cat,

"Meow... hie!" *("come here, cat"!)* (It still doesn't work!) And on and on it evolved over the millennia ... the human mind embracing new concepts while searching to express itself. To reverse the philosopher's adage, "The limits of our world are the limits of our language."

All this much time later, we're still imitating as we create new language to meet our word needs. All new words derive from older ones in one way or another. Marketing focus groups research sounds we associate with positive feelings. It is no coincidence that **Xanax makes you feel "relaxed."** And when detectives needed a new word for **"to follow closely behind a suspect,"** they didn't have to look farther than the **"tail"** of the dog to get an idea, and 'voila!' we had a new verb. People who are easily duped were tagged **'gullible'** by a clever wordsmith **connecting the "dupee" with the sneaky and deceptive characteristics of the seagull,** for the gain of a new adjective.

But there is relatively little **onomatopoeia** among the slew of new words we see every year. The daily comics were, in the 1950's, a great new source, among them a favorite, **"boing...the sound of a coiled spring being released."** Lewis Carroll's **"galumph... (1871) to move in a clumsy, ponderous or noisy manner"** is another.

Poets and songwriters delight us with their artful use of word sounds that, together, create a mood or feeling. These are sometimes referred to as **onomatopoeic poems.** Edgar Alan Poe was a master of the form. In his poem, "The Bells," written within earshot of Fordham University's church tower bells in the Bronx, he coined the word **tintinnabulation...a ringing or tinkling sound.** Using the word "bells" repeatedly and their various sounds, he celebrates the course of his love's life from their joyful courtship on a sleigh ride **("tinkle, tinkle, tinkle")** to his mourning her death **("tolling, tolling, tolling.")**

In this holiday season, if you are awakened by "such a clatter that you spring from your bed to see what's the matter" you may hear a familiar **onomatopoeic**-style stanza from *"Twas the Night before Christmas"*...

"Now Dasher! Now, Dancer! Now, Prancer and Vixen!/ On, Comet! on, Cupid! on, Donder and Blitzen!/ To the top of the porch! To the top of the wall!/ Now dash away! Dash away! Dash away all!"

The lines, with their reindeer names, verbs, and punctuation, work together to create a sense of excitement, movement, and **clatter.** (And you can see how that upstart, Rudolph, sooo never fit in!)

Enjoy the myriad sounds of the holiday season. Notice the mood they create...**(Ho-ho-ho!)** and see if you can identify a fresh **onomatopoeia** among them. The current list from **achoo to zoom** should welcome a newcomer.

Potlatch

THE **POTLATCH tradition of giving** practiced by the Kwakiutl and other Indian tribes of the Northwest includes **re-gifting.** In that tradition, I'd like to share several holiday gifts from friends, my attempt to redistribute the wealth of words I recently received.

First, a precious gift of "The Poems of William Cullen Bryant" published by THE HERITAGE PRESS in 1947, found at Bargain Books in Key West, and inscribed "Merry Christmas to Katharine, 1948, from Mother and Dad," includes the beautiful poem of nature, **"Thanatopsis."** Written when Bryant was only 17, it is a meditation on death. The title word is from the Greek *thantos* **... death** and *opsis* **... sight.** Reflective, yes, but not at all maudlin, it opens: "To him who in the love of Nature holds/Communion with her visible forms, she speaks/A various language..."

"The Word Museum, The Most Remarkable English Words Ever Forgotten" by Jeffrey Kacirk, 2000, Simon and Schuster, given by a dear friend who said she found it behind a row of shelved books, "clearly destined to be yours" opens with **abracadabrant ... marvelous or stunning** and **aflunters ... in a state of disorder** ("her hair was all aflunters.") Each of its 224 pages has at least one word I want to lobby dictionary editors to bring back. They don't make words like that any more! And how about **mawmsey ... sleepy; stupid, as from lack of rest or over-drinking.**

From an artist friend, I received "The Book of Hard Words" by David Bramwell, 2008, Ivy Press. This little jewel, a visual dictionary, defines, gives the etymology, and provides an example of usage for only one word per page! Each word is charmingly illustrated to provide what is called the "Read it-See it-Know it-Use it system." **Matroclinous ... taking after one's mother** (from Latin ***mater*** and Greek ***klinein*** ... **to learn)** and **echopraxia ... the compulsion to repeat or imitate the movements and postures of those around one** (from Greek ***echo*** ... **repeat** and ***praxia*** ... **action)** are among the entries. This gift included a very special artist-made bookmark.

On December 26, I celebrated **Kwanzaa** at a service led by Rev. Randy Becker at the UU church in Key West. This Pan-African American holiday centers around a consideration of "The Seven Principles" which reaffirm the dignity of the human person in community. Each is expressed in a single **Swahili** word, **Swahili** being the most universal of the African languages. From a word perspective, it was the sixth principle, **kuumba ... creativity,** that caught my attention. I wondered if it might be related to **Kumbaya**, the Joan Baez/ Peter, Paul and Mary folk song title we've all sung since the '60s on we-are-one-in-spirit occasions. But, no, **kumbaya ... "come by here,"** I learned, is from **Gullah, a creole pidgin dialect spoken by former slaves in the Sea Islands of South Carolina and Georgia.** Originally an African-American spiritual title, it dates to the 1920s.

Sometime back, a friend e-mailed suggesting I write a column on **onomatopoeia**, and offered **borborygmus ... the sound of intestinal rumbling**. I'm sorry I forgot to include it last month...it's a terrific example dating back to the Greeks and supports the theory that onomatopoeic or imitative words may have been the first uttered. This word lay in waiting for more than two millennia before getting a second job in plumbing. "All the toilets and waterpipes in the house had been suddenly seized with **borborygmic** convulsions," wrote Nabokov in 1969 in "Ada."

"Old Possum's Book of Practical Cats" is a wonderful gift from a loving friend. T.S. Eliot's book of poetry was the basis of "CATS," the second longest running musical in Broadway history. In the last stanza of "The Naming of Cats" I jumped with delight on a word I didn't know: "When you notice a cat in profound meditation,/The reason, I tell you, is always the same:/His mind is engaged in a rapt contemplation/Of the thought, of the thought, of the thought of his name:/His ineffable effable/**Effanineffable**/Deep and inscrutable singular Name."

Down the rabbit hole I went trying to find its meaning, or to discern the poet's creativity with words...(did I see the word 'feline' embedded anagrammatically in **effanineffable**?) Finally, the "Urban Dictionary" clued me in: **non-screwable; used by asexuals to describe themselves!!** It seems that 'effa' means 'the eff word' used more in days when people were less reluctant to cuss. Eliot used it as a prefix to emphasize the word ineffable! Because it's as unique as they are, asexuals adopted it in a sense that suited. The UD had another word that employs the same construction, **effanepic ... descriptive of anything with a high degree of epic qualities.**

I'm tempted to wish you an **effanepic** New Year full of great memories in the making!

Summer Catch

MENTALLY SEARCHING for an image that would serve to capture the feeling of this past fine Summer for me, I recalled spending afternoons at the beach on Long Island Sound watching fishermen net bait fish. It's an activity that has endured without change for thousands of years. That image from *this* Summer could be used to illustrate a Bible story.

It also serves as a metaphor for how I gathered words here and there...

On vacation in Stonington, Maine, I attended a benefit concert of folk and fiddle songs by *Archipelago*, a group of four very talented musician/singers. Geoff Warner rendered a wonderful song he wrote, **"Pronoia."** The word virtually jumped into my net! Geoff told me it was originally defined in the 70's as "a state of mind" by John Perry Barlow, a longtime songwriter for *Grateful Dead*. Recently it was used by well-known horoscope columnist, Rob Brezsny, as his book title, **"Pronoia is the Antidote for Paranoia: How All of Creation is Conspiring to Shower You with Blessings."** I hope the song, the book, and the concept go viral. Our world needs more pronoia and less paranoia. Let's spread the word! ..."**Pronoia"** is not yet used by enough of us to make it into the dictionaries.

An enthusiastic participant in my "Poetry Appreciation" group presented "Travel" ... "I should like to rise and go/Where the golden apples grow;" ... from Robert Louis Stevenson's collection, "A Child's Garden of Verses." I was carried back to my own youthful dreams of exotic experiences by the line, "swinging in a **palanquin;"** (pronounced **pal-an-keen**). This Javanese to Portuguese to English word is an **East Asian covered litter, carried on poles on the shoulders of two or four bearers.** By the time I was borne on one in Dacca, East Pakistan, (now Bangladesh) in the 60's, I found it bumpier than a Checker cab on a Manhattan Street, and so labor intensive, I felt very uneasy. That's how dreams sometimes go!

David Foster Wallace, in a 1997 review of John Updike's "Toward the End of Time," described the author as suffering from **"ontological despair"... a feeling that there's no worthwhile reason for being (based on 'ontology'...the branch of philosophy that deals with being).** The phrase was used to describe Wallace himself after he committed suicide in 2008 at the age of 46. I've long wondered if there might be a single word which could stand-in for that phrase, "ontological despair," and this summer came across one that comes close in a 1923 Dictionary list of German words which have come into English: **weltschmerz ... world weariness.**

"A Nation of **Scofflaws**" is the title of Part 2 of Ken Burns' excellent mini-series "Prohibition." **Scofflaw... simply scoff+ law...** has a nice quirky etymology...seems there was a contest in Boston in 1923 to come up with a word to define **"a lawless drinker of illegally made**

or illegally obtained liquor." Two of the 25,000 entries tied to win with the word we now apply to a person who willfully disregards *any* law. Example/confession: When I was taking literature courses at Baruch College in Manhattan many years ago, and always late for class, I had a favorite tiny illegal parking space on Lexington Ave. The floor of my VW "Beetle" was littered with dozens of unpaid parking tickets. I wonder if Ken would be interested in serializing "He Was A Hippie-Scofflaw."

Much as I respect and love to taste artisanal cheeses, I was not aware of "the evangelical zeal....among hard-core fanatics of fromage." As Brian Ralph, the "cave manager" at Murray's in Manhattan explained in the NYT (10/5/11) **affinage (a French word new to English) is the careful practice of ripening cheese.** The **affineur** prevents many of the problems that can occur if the temperature and humidity are not just right and the cheese does not develop the proper mold. Needless to say, there are skeptics who feel it's no more than a marketing gimmick, and parents who worry that their kids might aspire to be cave managers!

Making Sense of
Jabberwocky

I WAS MINDING my Ps and Qs recently, when I ventured upon "**portmanteau words**," that wonderful lexical key which opened the door to the creation of hundreds of new words since 1871, courtesy of Lewis Carroll. **Each is a blend of two or more words, their sounds and meanings combined.**

In his _Through the Looking-Glass_, Carroll has Humpty Dumpty explain the concept to Alice, "You see, it's like a portmanteau...there are two meanings packed up into one word." (**Portmanteau** is a French word, (carry+cloak) carried over to English, and currently called a "suitcase," which is designed in two halves, but combines into one.)

Carroll's genius gave us "**slithy**" (pronounced "sly-thee," he insisted) from "lithe and slimy" and "**mimsy**" from "miserable and flimsy" and my favorite, "**frumious,**" describing the "fuming and furious" Bandersnatch in the nonsense poem, _Jabberwocky_.

Victorians were besotted with Alice, as we are today with Harry Potter. Well-read, language-proud Englishmen made creating them fashionable, and "portmanteau words" proliferated.

Most were "**nonce words**," neo-logisms made up on the spot or for an occasion, but some went on to enter the standard vocabulary. Within a relatively short while, we were breathing **"smog,"** eating **"brunch"** and overnighting at **"motels."**

Today we generally call them **"hybrid words."** But technically, a "hybrid word" is composed of elements from different languages, e.g., **"pescalator ... a conveyor belt used on fish farms to move fish, as they grow, from one tank to another."** So I'm advocating for not letting go of "portmanteau" or the memory of Lewis Carroll.

Think of the lexical wealth he spawned: "bionic" (biology+electronic), "humongous" (huge+monstrous), "motorcade" (motor+cavalcade), "outpatient" (outside+patient), "palimony" (partner+alimony), "sitcom" (situation+comedy), and "telegenic" (television+photogenic), to name a few from a long list.

What name might Tanganyika and Zanzibar have used when they merged in 1964, without the portmanteau concept that suggests **"Tanzania?"**

How could we have survived these past twenty years, our political sense of humor intact, without **"Billary,"** and how would we cross the Channel without the **"Chunnel?"**

Portmanteau words pour out of our creative brains as we face new situations... **"Spanglish"** and **"Chinglish"** and **"Hinglish"** and **"Ponglish"** are heard in the melting pots of English speaking nations that continue to lure peoples of the world. **"Sporks"** and **"knorks"** are designed to make our cutlery choices simpler. And **"e-mail"** is making snail mail obsolete!

Erin Mc Kean, former Editor of the OED, in her new Wall Street Journal column, "Week in Words," recently reported that in the 1970s, Oliver, a chimp who walked upright, was suspected of being a **"humanzee"** until DNA testing proved otherwise.

So what can we make of Carroll's choice of a title for his nonsense poem in *Through the Looking Glass*? The clue is in the **"-wocky"** part of the word; it's from **"wocor"** an old Anglo-Saxon word meaning **"offspring or fruit."** There may have been a lesson intended: jabber often produces useful language as its offspring.

Alice herself said of *Jabberwocky*, "It seems very pretty but it's rather hard to understand. Somehow it seems to fill my head with ideas ..."

Jabber away!

It's Greek to Me!

THE OTHER DAY, following a talk I'd given, a word enthusiast raised her hand and asked, "Why do you feel **entomology** is so important?" I responded, deadpan, "Because they say **insects** will one day dominate the earth." She blushed as the audience laughed. But I am all too familiar with that mistake. I apologized to her for my smart-aleck response. Until I really got into **etymology, the study of the origin of words,** I hesitated in my reach for the correct one of those two words myself.

Among the nearly 500 **"–ologies," (Greek suffix for "the study of")** listed in the dictionary, many are difficult to remember or distinguish from another. **Cosmetology (cosmetics)** and **cosmology (the cosmos, the origins of the universe)** or **ethology (animal behavior)** and **etiology (the origins of disease)** could hardly be more different in meaning. Yet the words are similar enough in their look or sound that we blunder ceaselessly and tend to avoid using them. Too bad!

One of the banes of my existence is that favorite word of writers waxing philosophical, a word I really like but, ironically, can never remember: **epistemology (the study of the origins of human knowledge)**. I have to look it up *every* time, but I know one day it will stick.

Our problem, it seems to me, is most acute when the front part of the word is Greek as well. It's so much easier to say, "He **studies fish ... or spiders**" than to risk, "He's an **icthyologist** ... or an **arachnologist.**" If the root is a familiar word, even when of Greek origin, like **anesthesia**, we have little problem. Or if the word is thought of without regard to its being in two parts like **anthology (literally, "a gathering of similar flowers"),** or **archaeology**, it presents no challenge.

In modern times, many areas of scientific inquiry have had **"–ology"** added to them and work fine in our everyday language because we understand the root, as in **climatology** and **angelology.**

In American humor, we add all kinds of things up front of "-ology" to get a laugh or to be sarcastic, e.g., "I spend all this dough on tuition and my kid is studying **"beerology."** Or, when asked to take out the trash: "What am I... a **"garbologist?"**

As problematic as **"-ologies"** may be, English owes Greek a big debt: almost 30% of the 80,000 words educated people use derive from Greek.

Back to the intended question, I feel **"etymology"** is important because language is inextricable from history. Historic events, periods, and trends bring changes that are reflected in the words/language we use. Investigating the origin of a word can serve as the threshold to the study of some interesting aspect of history.

There are, of course, major events like the Norman Conquest that resulted in our language adapting to become one-third French...and a big story there!

On a smaller scale, consider two words: **pajamas** and **shirtwaist.** Also spelled **pyjamas**, it derives from the Persian *peyjama*, and was incorporated, via Hindustani, into English, during **the Raj, the period of British colonial rule in South Asia (1857-1947),** along with many other words including khaki, dungarees, and pundit. A parent might use the time of putting on the kids' pajamas for a short **etymology**/history lesson, "Do you know where that word came from?"

The word **shirtwaist, a woman's upper body garment,** fell out of use after the deadly and much publicized **Triangle Shirtwaist Factory fire** one hundred years ago. **"Blouse"** replaced it, and the ILGWU was born. **Etymology** in the making!

Skeleton Bones in Your Language?

A RECENT *NY Times/Arts* headline, **"Once More, Revisiting A Queen Yet Again"** is a playful **double-redundancy**, amplified to open a Janet Maslin review of yet another book about Anne Boleyn. Seeing it, I decided to write a piece on "redundancy" that would trace my own arc from a grade school nun's dictum,

"it's unnecessary, so don't use one *ever!*" to my current libertine attitude, "if it's fun, use one!" Along the way, I realized that my favorite food, **tuna fish**, was a redundancy, and, at one point, that I was in the euphemistically termed **"redundancy business"**, counseling **laid-off employees**.

I hear redundancies all day long, **"My son is wearing an earring in his ear."** (and oxymoronic replies, **"Thank God, he's not wearing it in his tongue."**), and read them in serious literature, like this from Sandra Steingraber in January's *The SUN*, "The house sparrow is a biblical species. It originated in the Middle East and is now **ubiquitous all over the world.**"

Here are several that may wave a redundancy flag at you in conversation: **safe haven, tiny bit, passing fad, head honcho, old proverb.**

Wrapping one's arms around Google results for **"redundancy"** is like trying to embrace a giant octopus! Basically, **"redundant"** means **superfluous**. It's been forever associated with language, meaning **unnecessarily wordy,** as in **"audible to the ear."** Indeed, its synonyms: **"tautology"** comes from **Greek, tauto-** (same), **-logy** (word), and **"pleonasm"** means using **more than enough language in speaking or writing.**

But over the centuries the word has proven to have great elasticity. Not only writers, but engineers, chemists, logicians, and, as per my own experience above, Human Resources professionals, have stretched its meaning and applied it to anything that duplicates something else. **Now** that **redundancy applies to concepts rather than strictly to words,** now that it is used to convey any superfluity or duplication, we see it used more and more. It's a great example of "living language," of "etymology in action."

But we must not be hasty in stretching the word! For example, the human appendix, once called "vestigial," which it is, came to be described as "redundant" which it is not. Its importance as part of the lymphatic system that fights infections in the body was discovered in 1997.

The concept of redundancy is *very* fashionable. Eager writers use **"a bit redundant"** and I ponder whether that's the linguistic equivalent of **"a little pregnant!"** In one sitting with the morning papers recently, I read the comic strip, "Shoe": a character is given the school assignment to **write a sentence that illustrates a redundancy** and he types, **"There was a full moon**

over the nudist colony," and an article by A. O. Scott: **"... Meryl Streep's 16th Oscar nomination ... seemed both richly merited and a bit redundant."** In these cases, the word is stretched to the sense of, **"it goes without saying."**

Unintended redundancies are common when we use acronyms. How often have you heard or seen: **please RSVP** ("please" is redundant as 's'il vous plait' means 'please'), and **ATM machine** ("machine" is redundant as the M stands for it). **PIN number** is another familiar one.

Most important, I think, is to be so familiar with **redundancies** that you recognize one when you see or hear it, and that when you use one, you are fully aware you are doing so. They can be great fun ... used well to make a point or to make your listener laugh. Consider this redundant bit of reportage attributed to a radio announcer, **"The robbery was committed by a pair of identical twins. Both are said to be aged about twenty."** Intentional or not, it's a brilliant and subtle example of the form.

To sum up, I want to say, "My nun could have had more fun." And I don't believe that's an oxymoron!

BAWDY! ... With Familiar Words

ERNEST HEMINGWAY once said, **"All my life I've looked at words as though I were seeing them for the first time."** We readily nod our heads ... it sounds good. Yet most of us treat **familiar words** all too casually. It does not occur to us, for example, to look up "right" or "humor" or "mimic," because we *know* what they mean. We go to the dictionary mostly when we come across a word whose meaning we can't begin to guess. But we are missing some **great lexical adventures**.

That Hemingway quote made me aware of this tendency in myself. Determined to fight it, I created an acronym, **BAWDY!** for the refrigerator door, where all wisdom resides. **Become A Word Detective, You!** it reminds me constantly. And my dictionary and I began to keep steady company.

Eventually, a **familiar word** like **"robot"** would seem worth looking up, and **prove itself to be an etymological gem.** I got in the habit of snooping around familiar words to see what lurked in their backgrounds. I wrote a poem about it: (please read aloud)

Familiar Words
Have you ever said, or read,
a word you've heard a million times,

but now, somehow,
you stop on a dime and mime
its sound around in your mouth?

You grab the D book and look it up,
and the beauty of its def or duty
comes through to you
for the first time and you say, "Hey,"
"this is really, truly interesting!"

Recently, I shared this with my "Crazy About Words" class and randomly selected **"amuse"** for the group to investigate further.

We noted its earliest recorded use in Middle French in the late 15th century, **amuser, ("a," to cause + "muser" to ponder.)** Later it was used in the sense of **divert from serious business,** but with a negative connotation. By the 18th century it had come into English more in the sense of **to entertain.**

We were surprised to see it in "The Student's Dictionary" which my class purchases and distributes to about 300 Third Graders every Fall, defined as **"to cause to smile."** And we Googled it to find that its hottest use for the past fifteen years or so is in the phrase **amuse-bouche,** (literally, to amuse the mouth), **a bite-sized hors d'oeuvre served to restaurant patrons as a greeting from the chef de cuisine.**

But our best find came when we looked up **"muse"** and found that it derived from the **Greek Muses, nine goddesses begat by Zeus and Mnemosyne, Goddess of Memory, who were the inspirations**

for the arts, poetry, music, dance, literature, history and astronomy. These were the diversions, the entertainment of the ancients.

The word comes down to us through the ages, its meaning evolving with the culture, and now used in a much expanded sense of diversion. The Muse-Goddesses might frown on our **wax museums and amusement parks** but *they* are the ultimate source of the whole business of amusement.

We word-crazy people had indeed become word detectives.

BAWDY!

How We Love Linguistic Twists!

IN 1954, *Harper's Magazine* published an essay, "The Death of Lady Mondegreen" by Sylvia Wright. She told the story of her mishearing a line from a 17th century Scottish ballad when she was a young girl. She remembered, "They hae slain the Earl O' Moray/ *And Lady Mondegreen.*" She felt deeply for the woman as she imagined her bravely dying on the battlefield alongside her husband. Ms. Wright fashioned a personal heroine of her Lady Mondegreen and never forgot her. Many years later, she saw the ballad in print, and read unbelievingly, "*.... And laid him on the green.*"

In the 1954 essay, she mourned the loss of her fictional heroine and ensconced her permanently in the English lexicon. She wrote, "the point about what I shall hereafter call **mondegreens**, since no one else has thought up a word for them, is that they are better than the original."

It took a while, but **mondegreen (the mishearing or misinterpretation of a phrase as a result of near-homophony, in a way that gives it a new meaning)** was finally included in the 2000 edition of *Webster's Collegiate Dictionary*. It is most commonly applied to a line in a poem or a lyric in a song.

I have wanted to write about this phenomenon for several years, but couldn't remember the word (a column-killer from the get-go!), until Anu Garg covered it recently in his highly recommended A.Word.A.Day feature at Wordsmith.org. About the same time Ms. Wright was coining the word, my nine year old sister was singing, *"...leave your pickle vats* (fickle past) *behind you"* to the tune of Patti Page's hit song, "Cross Over The Bridge," leaving our word-loving family laughing and wishing there was a word for such a funny mistake.

With or without their nomenclature, wonderful **mondegreens** pop-up all over the place. Malachy McCourt's memoir, *"A Monk Swimmin'"* derives from his incorrect childhood repetition of a line from the "Hail Mary"..."blessed art thou *amongst women."*

School kids reciting the Pledge of Allegiance are known to intone a phrase misheard as *"...one nation underdog, with liver, tea, and justice for all."*

In 1943, long before Ms. Wright's naming it, Milton Drake wrote a novelty song, (a **deliberate mondegreen,** we call it now) that had a whole nation in need of a little fun, singing:

Mairzy doats and dozy doats and liddle lamzy divey

A kiddley divey too, wooden shoe

If the words sound queer and funny to your ear,

A little bit jumbled and jivey,

Sing "Mares eat oats and does eat oats, and little lambs eat ivy;

A kid'll eat ivy too, wouldn't you?"

Since the 1990s introduction of CC (closed captioning) for which a computer instantly translates audio into visual words on a screen for the hearing-impaired, or in noisy environments, there has been a happy surge in **mondegreen** creation. My favorite is that reported by a hearing-impaired woman whose friend was talking to her on her adapted phone about using a juicer to make a healthful drink. At one point she said, "You just throw out the pulp and keep the juice." It displayed on the screen as, "*...throw out the Pope and keep the Jews.*"

Among other forms of linguistic error that entertain, delight, and confound us, are **spoonerisms (also called marrowskys), malapropisms, and Freudian slips** (each an **eponym** derived respectably from Rev. Archibald Spooner, Polish Count Marrowsky, Mrs. Malaprop, the main character in Sheridan's 1775 play, *The Rivals,* and Sigmund Freud).

Have fun recognizing them...and see if you can identify the intentional linguistic error in this column!

June Bugs and Other Cute Things

TODAY, WE TOAST **June Bugs**, the genus **phyllophaga, (from two Greek words, phaga-eating + phyllo-leaves)**, not because of their propensity to eat everything in your garden this month, but because their name, as it rolls off the tongue, has delighted the ears and piqued the imaginations of so many language-loving humans. "June bugs" or "Junebugs" has lent its cute name to song and movie titles, fictional characters, a tropical cocktail made with rum and melon liqueur, a 1908 Curtis-design aircraft, and to Dale Earnhardt, Jr. of NASCAR fame as a nickname.

A quintessential American expression, "**gung-ho**," **originated as two Chinese characters meaning 'work together,'** and was the name of a Chinese workers' co-operative. The sound and its meaning was picked up by a US Marine Major in the Pacific in 1943. Anxious to boost the team spirit of his men, he adopted the term, **gung-ho**, which swept quickly through the Marine Corps. It was used as the title of a movie starring Randolph Scott and Robert Mitchum later the same year. After the war, its usage broadened in American culture to mean **highly enthusiastic or dedicated.**

Speaking of Americanisms, former Poet Laureate, Billy Collins, wrote a wonderful, funny poem titled "Le Chien" in which a tipsy narrator engages a dog in a one-way conversation late at night on a street in Paris. The narrator attempts to explain a list of phrases including "corn dog," "white walls," "tag sale," "helmet laws," and **"the March of Dimes,"** as the dog stares with "dark-brown, adoring eyes." The last on this list made *me* howl... I suppose because it is generically different from the others in the list and came as a surprise. It was originally called the "National Foundation for Infantile Paralysis" by its founder, President Franklin D. Roosevelt. The much catchier **"March of Dimes"** came later, thanks to vaudeville star, Eddie Cantor, who hosted a 1938 benefit he named as a take on the popular contemporary newsreel series, "The March of Time."

A recent "Google a Day" quiz asked, "How many times larger is a million than a **myriad**?" I had only known this word as meaning **a very large but indefinite number**, but learned that it was the ancient Greek equivalent of 10,000, their largest number. Today, **our largest named number is 'googol' ... a 1 followed by one hundred zeros**. Ironically, "Google" was named by its founders in a misspelling of **"googol"** intended to signify that the company wanted to provide huge quantities of information to its **myriad** customers.

I saw the word **myriad** again the same day in this bit of wry humor from Jennifer Egan's new sci-fi short story, *"Black Box,"* released last month by *The New Yorker* as serial tweets. Each sentence is a "mental dispatch" from a high-tech female spy operating in the Mediterranean: "If you wish to avoid physical intimacy, (with her abductor, as he hurries her to the waterfront) the sight of a speedboat will bring relief, despite the **myriad** new problems it presents." I loved the story, as I did her 2011 Pulitzer Prize winning novel, *A Visit from The Goon Squad.*

Had I seen the word **shambolic** standing alone, I might have guessed it to be associated with an Eastern philosophy, akin to 'shamanic' perhaps. But, in the context of Thomas Beller's sentence in a recent NYT article about his being a writer who divides his time between NYC and New Orleans, it defined itself. "...I came up with a theory that New Orleans was like the New York of the 1970s ... ungentrified, **shambolic**, chaotic in ways bad and good, cheap, terrifying, a place hospitable to whimsy." Its first recorded use was in 1970, and it is still regarded as British slang meaning **chaotic or disorganized, a glorious mess**. I don't know why it is taking so long to have it acknowledged as a proper adjective derived from **shambles**; there is no other.

Your bonus "June bug:" **quagmire**...is 2 words put together, each meaning the same thing...**a marsh or a bog**...a redundancy within itself! I can't wait to use its adjective, **quaggy**, the next time I step onto my over-watered lawn.

"Inkhorn Terms"

IT'S A SHAME that this noun phrase is no longer in common use. I discovered it recently in "The Word Museum, ... The Most Remarkable English Words Ever Forgotten," by Jeffrey Kacirk. I was relieved to know it, because I have long felt at a loss for what to call all **the wonderful words, phrases, and expressions writers come up with** to make our language more vivid. I have, at times, referred to them as **"writerly" inventions**, but that's not a name that sticks as "inkhorn terms" once did.

The words that writers and speakers invent or derive to enhance and color our communications, ought to have a name. If the **"tips of shoelaces"** deserve **"aglets" (from French, *aguille* for needle)**, then surely a noble handle is due what were once called "**inkhorn terms**."

I understand how it faded from use. Who knows anymore what the heck an **"inkhorn"** is? ... even "ink" is not understood as it once was ... perhaps better known now as the fluid an octopus employs for defense than as the medium of writers. **Animal horns were used, like powderhorns, to carry quills and ink and were once a symbol of the writer's trade**.

"Inkhorn term" was originally used derisively in the late 1500s, (during the transition from Middle English to Modern English), by purists defending the Anglo-Saxon language against the incursion of Latin, Greek, and French words being introduced by writers to combat the limitations of the largely four-letter-word AS vocabulary. *"The most ancient English wordes are of one syllable, so that the more monosyllables you use, the truer Englishman you shall seem, and the less you shall smell of the **Inkhorne**." George Gascoigne, 1575.*

The purists agreed that the language needed more words, but thought they could be created out of what people already knew. Had they prevailed, we might today be using simple, derivative words such as **'gleeman' for musician, 'inwit' for conscience, 'yeartide' for anniversary, 'starlore' for astronomy, and 'speechcraft' for grammar.** But language progressives won the day and a flood of Renaissance-era inkhorn words were embraced. Among them: **anonymous, catastrophe, expectation, lunar, and pathetic.**

Modern English continues to expand as it begs the imaginations of people who love language, borrows from other languages, and steals outright from everywhere. **"Hedonists" were simply "pleasure seekers"** until someone went for the Greek root in the mid 1800s. **"Humongous" combined "huge" and "monstrous"** on a US College campus in 1967 and spread like wildfire into everyday use. **"Wildfire"** is an invented word that relies on the double meaning of 'wild' for its sense; in Spanish, one has to say "incendios en areas naturales" and even that long phrase doesn't capture the rage involved.

Because of this expansive quality born of the "Inkhorne Controversy," English today is the "go-to" language for people around the world seeking common ground in communication. The origin of **"dust bunny"** cannot be traced beyond the fact of its US origin, but you might well hear the term in the middle of a sentence spoken in another language. Similarly, **"control freak," "bunker mentality," "brain trust" and "shazam"** are modern terms originated by writers, but lacking a word that defines them.

I believe that if all of my "Crazy About Words" readers put our minds to it, we'll come up with a good idea for a word or phrase that redefines these "inkhorn terms" for modern times. Then I'll work to spread it around among dictionary editors. So, let's try some **crowdsourcing.**

Words We Seldom Speak

A RECENT *New Yorker* cartoon depicts a mother imploring her teenage daughter, "Try and tell me what's bothering you, dear---use your **S.A.T. words**." Even before I stopped laughing, I knew I had to do this column!

The child might respond, "I suffer **quotidian** depression because my **academic colleagues** do not regard me as **estimable**. They say I am **querulous**." What she means is, "I'm down in the dumps all the time because my classmates don't like me. They say I'm always complaining."

Only **quotidian ... daily** is not on a list of 5,000 top SAT words I Googled. It's a word I like very much, but hesitate to use in conversation, because a) I'm worried that "quotidian" is not used *exactly* the way "daily" is, but I'm not certain of the difference, and b) I want to be considerate of my **interlocutor**.

David Brooks, commenting on the recent election on PBS, stumbled in pronouncing the word **cavil... minor objection.**

He blushed, then stammered with charm and humor, through three possible pronunciations, acknowledging that he didn't know if the accent went on the first or second syllable (it's the first), and whether the "i" should be pronounced as in "it" or as in "niche" (as in "it"). This is another reason many of us don't speak words we learned for our SATs and see mostly in print.

For me, **promontory ... a headland** falls into this category... I used to mangle it, in part because I spelled it with an extra "o," as though three "o"s were not enough! Finally, I stopped using it! Check it out on, www.howjsay.com a free online pronunciation dictionary. (If I lived on the northern end of Great Salt Lake in Utah in the Promontory Mountains, I'd be accustomed to saying the word!)

Some words we don't utter, because we worry about sounding pretentious. Once an altar boy, I've always loved the word **acolyte** but I use **assistant or follower** in conversation. And how about **prolix ... long, drawn out, using too many words?** ("His essay was **prolix.**") It's simpler to use "**verbose or long winded**" in conversation. Besides, it doesn't sound like an adjective to me. My first reaction when I come across it is that it's a chemical term!

A recent NYT opinion column critical of motivational speaker Tony Robbins said, "... his trademark smile starts to resemble a

rictus." ... a mouth gaping open, a fixed grimace. This word too feels most appropriate for print, where the reader has a chance to recall it or look it up, rather than leaving a listener fixing a rictus on his face.

Misanthropic ... hating mankind seems a quintessential SAT word from the list. Faced with expressing the idea verbally, except possibly at an academic gathering, most of us are apt to say, "He has no use for people."

My high school Latin teacher, Brother Alfonse Patrick, a huge Hibernian with a love of the language as big as his penchant for teaching it the old fashion way, impressed on me over four years that, if you studied Latin, you could easily determine the meaning of any English word having a Latin root. Came my NYS English Regents exam, we were asked to define **obsequious** by using it in a sentence. Brother Patrick whacked me on the head with the Latin textbook when he learned of my response: "After you take a shower, the **obsequious** thing to do is dry yourself." Well, "sequere" does mean "to follow" as in "sequence"... but I was ignoring the "ob-" which changes it to **"following in a slavish way."** Needless to say, I cannot to this day say the word without feeling funny.

In real life, our cartoon child, aware of the power of **monosyllabic** responses to irk parents, probably would have answered her mother, **"Whaaat??"** Then, having been reminded that her SATs are coming up, she goes to a great website, www.freerice.com where she has fun practicing her vocabulary through multiple-choice questions. You can too. For every correct answer, the site donates ten grains of rice to the UN World Food Program. How cool is that!

Ugh! Slugs

SOMETIMES A VERY ordinary word goes to extraordinary ends to get your attention ...

I walked out for a bit of fresh air and a look at the coming-on moon before going to bed one hot and humid Saturday night in August two years ago. On my way back in I had to sidestep to avoid squishing **slugs** which had appeared on the slate walkway during the five minutes I was gone.

If you've ever stepped on one you'd remember. It's more like slipping on a banana peel than crushing a bug, and I muttered, "Damn things ... you could really break your neck."

I counted six of them in the course of a few feet **(a "slugfest!")** and stopped to notice how each moved ever so slowly, or just lay there in its slime. They seemed to have no other destination or purpose than to get under my feet, after feasting on the leaves in my garden.

Then I observed that they resembled apostrophes, and felt a little better about them, because I'm a big fan of punctuation. Which got me thinking about the word ... "s-l-u-g". Nice little four-letter guy ... an anagram of "lugs" ... too bad there isn't a word "glus"... and what might it mean if there were?

Besides being the name for these slimy, slippery creatures that no one can warm up to, **"slug"** is a verb and a noun meaning "punch," as in, "... then he slugged the guy." And, of course, we call people who seem lazy and unmotivated "slugs" or **"sluggards"** ... no doubt derived from the characteristic **"sluggish"** movement of the lower form. Then, we have "slug" as a piece of metal, a blank, to be made into a bullet or a counterfeit coin. And, oh yes, there's a slug of water, or some other liquor.

It's interesting to speculate on the etymology, how over the centuries, these several meanings might have derived from one original idea of something slow and heavy. And it's fun to realize how we've built on this little word to get **sluggish, slugger, slugging average, and slugfest.**

It occurred to me that if you think of a slug as a **"snail,"** to which it is very closely related, you instantly upgrade its image; not only does no one gag when you mention a snail, most people smile at their mental image of a mythic, self-reliant creature toting its mobile home along, looking, for all the world, like a moving Scotch tape dispenser. Or they picture delicious escargot bathing in garlicky butter.

My reverie ended with a chuckle as I realized how much time I'd spent on this word... a most unlikely subject. Most people would be waxing poetic over the magnificent moon while I'd been looking down at what must be pretty near the bottom of the evolutionary scale.

I was in for a pleasant surprise the very next morning when I grabbed the NYTimes "Week in Review." Verlyn Klinkenborg, a brilliant essayist whose attention to the tiniest details of life gives me such pleasure, opened "The Rural Life" on the editorial page as follows:

"I do not detest slugs. They are a perfectly valid life form. I discover them in the garden with no surprise or alarm. I expect to find them on the stone walk in the early morning, and I step around them, respectfully. But now I find them on the walls of the house, climbing up the doorjamb, climbing up the door as if they were going to pick the lock and come in out of the rain. In their form, their liquid drop-like appearance, they distill the essence of this appalling summer. It's as if the thunderheads – rising fungally above us – were raining slugs."

What a nice coincidence, I thought, to be seeing analogies along with of one of my favorite writers ...

But how much coincidence can there be before it's called something else? I turned to the "Op-Eds" page in the same issue and Nicholas Kristof's column title jumped off the page, "How To Lick A Slug"!

His essay was a thoughtful lament of the fact that kids these days do not value and learn from being outdoors as they once did. He ends with this sentence:

"Time was... most kids knew that if you licked the underside of a banana slug, your tongue went numb. Better that than have them numb their senses staying cooped up inside."

And the next day's NYT crossword offered the clue "Mays" for which the answer was "slugger Willie"!

My imagination had been captured by "slug" to which I'd previously given no mind whatever. With its appearance now compared to a drop of water, a banana, and an apostrophe, the slug has great metaphorical potential for a wordsmith.

But was the Universe conspiring to tell me something more? Had it brought this lowliest of creatures and simplest of words dramatically to my attention for some good reason? Or was it just a coincidence?

The naturalist, William Burroughs, once said, "In the magical universe, there are no coincidences and there are no accidents." And Elizabeth Kubler-Ross adds, "All events are blessings given to us to learn from."

I thought about it and remembered that I'd recently had palpitations, for which the doctor offered, "You've got to remember to slow down."

The slugs were my reminder!

Quote, Unquote ... or, I Could Have Said That!

I CAN'T PUT the words together as well as he did, so I'll quote Nathaniel Hawthorne, **"Words ... so innocent and powerless as they are, as standing in a dictionary, how potent for good and evil they become, in the hands of one who knows how to combine them."**

Do you ever wish you might combine your words into bon mots so pithy and perfect that they'd echo for generations off the lips of millions? ... like, **"Practice makes perfect,"** an ancient Latin proverb, first used in the US by John Adams, or **"A bird doesn't sing because it has an answer, it sings because it has a song."** (Maya Angelou).

You owe it to yourself to post your well-expressed thoughts on Facebook, Twitter, or at least on the 'fridge,' the American family's kiosk for the exchange of wit and wisdom. Who knows what may come of it? To quote Edward Thorndike, American psychologist (1874-1949), **"Colors fade, temples crumble, empires.**

And Elbert Hubbard, American writer, philosopher and artist (1856-1915), may once have had this taped to his bathroom mirror, **"Be pleasant until ten o'clock in the morning and the rest of the day will take care of itself."**

It's great to keep a diary or journal, where your musings express your passions and pleasures. In this vein, Truman Capote said, **"To me, the greatest pleasure of writing is not what it's about, but the music the words make."** And Kahlil Gibran noted, **"Poetry is a deal of joy and pain and wonder, with a dash of the dictionary."**

The words of others sometimes resonate for us in a personally helpful way, and we use them (with attribution, of course!) as though they were our own. In this category I like, **"Doubt requires more courage than conviction does, and more energy."** (John Patrick Shanley, Author of "Doubt"); also, **"At its core, what holds the world together is love."** (Goethe), and **"Travelers, there is no path. Paths are made by walking."** (Antonio Machado, Spanish poet, 1875-1939.)

Some quotes tickle even as they give us pause to think: **"If God had been a liberal, we wouldn't have had the 10 Commandments...we'd have the 10 Suggestions."** (Malcolm Bradbury). **"I wish I didn't know now what I didn't know then."** (from 'Runnin' Against the Wind' song by Bohlen & Dieter). And, Maya Angelou again, **"I've learned that you can tell a lot about a person by the way he/she handles these three things: a rainy day, lost luggage, and tangled Christmas tree lights."**

For pure memorability, you can't beat this pair: **"Our conscience is the only incorruptible thing about us."** (Henry Fielding, 1707-1754, London magistrate, satirist, and creator of the picaresque *Tom Jones*), and

"There is no stronger army in all the world than an idea whose time has come." (Victor Hugo).

For all the wit and wisdom captured in these quotes, we know words can also be combined to do harm. Bullying is a criminal act. But, when Hamlet, in Act 2, Scene 2, responds, **"Words, words, words,"** he is reminding Lord Polonius that slanders are *only* words. As kids, we learned to chime the retort, **"Sticks and stones may break my bones, but names will never hurt me."**

Although they can indeed hurt, we must continually remind ourselves that, *whatever* the intention of words delivered, **"Actions speak louder ..."**

Some Ado About Prepositions

IF YOU'RE LIKE ME, this is the first, or at most the second time you've thought about prepositions since somewhere around sixth grade. And learning about them even then was a non-event, akin maybe to studying the teeth's role in chattering ... they happen automatically... what's to learn? Plenty, I've discovered, researching this column, if you really want to get into the subject.

But today I'll simply raise your consciousness enough so that when your Valentine coos, **"Little things mean a lot, sweetheart,"** you think prepositions. And you reply, "Yes, honey, **of, to** and **in** are among the ten most frequently used words in the English language."

And you hear back, "What are you talking **about?"**

You can't resist, "Honey, you are *stranding* **a preposition**. For sure you've been taught never to use one at the end of a sentence."

Although your honey has a this-is-the-Valentine-from-hell look in her eye, she blinks and rises to the occasion, "But remember even Winston Churchill made fun of *that* rule. **'This is the sort of English up with which I will not put,'** he said, to illustrate its awkwardness."

You're stunned by her knowledge and playfulness. And **apropos** of your loving concession, you share a bon mot Somerset Maugham once delivered, **"Usage is the only**

test. I prefer a phrase that is easy and unaffected to one that is grammatical."

You both swoon. You feel you're on the verge of 'living happily ever **after**,' and you say so, aware as you do that something is not exactly right in your grammatical thinking. "Let's go to *"Crazy About Words"* and learn a little more," you suggest.

After, while most frequently used as a preposition, is, in this case, an adverb. It modifies the verb 'living' in the phrase 'living happily ever after.'

A **preposition** is a word that links a noun or pronoun to other words in a sentence, in terms of time (the calm **after the storm)**, space (the dog chased **after the cat**), or logic (she is named **after her mother).** Together, the preposition and its complementary noun or pronoun are called a **prepositional phrase**; the full phrase is most commonly used as a noun, adjective, or adverb.

Prepositions are a **closed class** of words, meaning that we English speakers very seldom add to the list of about 130 of them. Our language evolves mostly by the addition and modification of nouns, adjectives, and verbs.

I once heard Calvin Trillin quip, when asked how he manages to get along in several foreign languages, "It's simple: I don't do verbs." I smile picturing him using pantomime to communicate action verbs on the streets of Barcelona, Berlin or Bologna...we've all played charades.

But prepositions, for all their apparent bitsiness, are one of the most difficult aspects of a language to learn, especially for non-native speakers. Among other challenges they present, prepositions are highly **polysemous ... with many nuances of meaning** ('after' has 6, 'in' has 8, 'to'-7, 'with'-10), to say nothing of the fact that most also serve as adjectives, adverbs, and occasionally nouns (He had an **in** with the boss.) These difficulties have caused **"an epidemic of prepositional anarchy"** says David Thatcher, author of "Saving Our Prepositions: A Guide for the Perplexed."

Listen carefully to a non-native speaker. You're more likely to hear errors in her or his choice of prepositions than in any of the other eight parts of speech. I have a friend from Poland who has settled on 'for' as her favorite fallback preposition in English; she uses it to cover 'in' 'at' and 'to'...("Say hello for (to) your mother." "I am looking for (at) your dog.") When I'm struggling along in French, Spanish, or Italian, I get lazy about prepositions and tend to use 'a' when I'm not sure, and my German is replete with 'auf.' I get lots of laughs!

The danger in selecting the wrong preposition is well illustrated by noting the difference in meaning between "They went hand **in** hand." and "They went hand **to** hand." And the merchandising potential of a little preposition is clear in a clever sign on a bakery door here in Key West, "Get your buns **in** here."

If perchance this **ado (to do)** has left you overly stimulated, you may want to sing along to **"The Preposition Song"** ... (many renditions available at YouTube.com).

Eating Poetry

I ATTENDED the week long Key West Literary Seminar and Workshop in January, entirely dedicated to Poetry this year in honor of Richard Wilbur, former Poet Laureate and Key West resident. At 89, he stood erect and read with a strong voice from his new book, from his poem, "A Measuring Worm," **"And I, too, don't know/Toward what undreamt condition/Inch by inch I go."**

The goosebumps came up, and I was reminded of a sentence from an essay by Carmine Starnino in January's *POETRY* magazine, "Nothing in my life matched that language and I rejoiced in its **acoustic plushness.**" He was referring with nostalgia to **"hallowed be thy name"** from the Lord's Prayer, his "first contact with poetry", which he regards as a **"packet of linguistic energy."**

I've been searching for a word, or a phrase like **"acoustic plushness"** for years! It so perfectly describes a combination of sound and rhythm, words so sensitively and beautifully put together that repeating them feels like eating ripe plums. When I was a boy, and even now, **"Once upon a time..."** casts a spell, makes me want to curl up and listen with my whole being, because it feels like a promise of acoustic plushness to follow. I think we all have those phrases, lines of poetry, or quotes from Shakespeare, words we love to say out loud, that make us shiver a bit when we do.

Here are two more that did that for me when read at the KW Literary Seminar:

-from "Fountain in the City" by Timothy Steele,
"the water climbed to a white crest, and fell,/plashy and heavy, to a metal shell/forever in a state of overflow/and then went dripping to the pool below."

-from "Cambridge, Great St. Mary's Church" by Rita Dove,
"...Music/pours through the blackened nave,/hollowing my bones to fit/the space it needs."

After three days of Seminar, I enrolled in one of the 4-day writing workshops offered, where I bore witness to the fact that, as Starnino says, **"poems live entirely inside their linguistic devices and designs ... the poet is someone for whom language gets the whole of his or her attention."** I had the pleasure of indulging myself in words for hours at a time!

At one point I found myself writing a poem likening life to a flower, and the line **"...thorns abound along the/stem, but give me (*nothing*) to fear."** Reading that line aloud you'll feel how choppy the second line sounds. The two- syllable "nothing" is the culprit ... a smooth, one syllable word is needed in its place ...but what? After much concentration, **"naught"** emerges. It's a word I'm quite certain I've not used since it meant "zero" in grade school, but here it is, a perfect substitute in this poem, and now one I will never forget! (Try reading it aloud with this substitution!)

When this wonderful week is almost done, I find a line from **"Eating Poetry"** by Mark Strand, one of the seven US Laureates on the program at the Key West Literary Seminar, which aptly describes my activity and feelings.

"Ink runs from the corners of my mouth./There is no happiness like mine./I have been eating poetry."

The Etymology of Two Popular Phrases

WE TOASTED a **blue moon** on New Year's Eve not too long ago. The phrase has a colorful origin dating to a 1528 anti-clerical **screed**, "If they say the moon is blue/we must believe that it is true."

As the Church was responsible for setting the date for Easter back then, the clergy had to keep track of the calendar dates on which the **lent moon**, the late Winter moon, and the **egg moon**, the early Spring moon, occurred. Every several years they came too early, for astronomical reasons now widely understood. As they wouldn't have Easter in February, the too-early lent moon was disregarded as false, and was declared to be a **"belewe"** moon, and the *next* one was designated the real lent moon.

But that Olde English word, **"belewe"** meant both **betrayer** (false) and **blue**, and therein lay the immortalizing opportunity seized in 1528 by that sacrilegious punster.

We don't know if he lost his head for his **play on words,** which depicted the clergy proposing such an absurdity as a **blue moon**, but **lexicographers regard his phrase as an etymological gem**, because it can be traced to a specific source almost 500 years old and its usage has been so continually documented through the centuries.

"Blue moon" stuck with a vengeance! While we think of it today as the second Full Moon to occur in a single calendar month, until 1946 it was always that extra "betrayer" fourth moon occurring in one of the thirteen-week seasons. Every 2.7 years on average, a **blue moon** interrupts the otherwise predictable progression of the moons whose seasonal, mythical names are all so enchanting.

Beyond its astronomical definition, **"once in a blue moon"** means **rarely** in our language even to those astrological heathens who don't know what a blue moon really is! And **blue moon** has inspired romantic songs, poetry, horror stories, and a name for thousands of bars and cafes around the world.

It is **a compelling phrase that has never been used literally** except following the eruption of Krakatoa in 1883 when, I've read, particles lingering in the air caused the moon to appear bluish for two years.

Another phrase I believe will live on even as the recollection of its origin fades is **soap opera.** Already many have forgotten or never known that the term had its origin in the sponsorship of daytime radio serials by soap companies. The very first **"soap"** was "Clara Lu 'n Em" sponsored by Super Suds which ran from 1930 to 1945.

The **defining element of a "soap" is the open-ended nature of the narrative,** concluding frequently with a "cliffhanger," but always, each day, with a promise that the story will be continued.

How will the phrase "soap opera" survive without soap now that "As the World Turns," the last daytime drama presented by Procter & Gamble, has gone off the air? Those dramas and our own real life dramas are now solidly entrenched in our vocabulary figuratively as "soap opera." It now remains the business of **etymologists** to document how the phrase came about.

(Many everyday phrases have interesting etymologies. You can check them out when they strike you simply by Googling them.)

It's up to you to remember that **you are the star of your own soap opera**, and that **only once in a blue moon does someone like you come along!**

Loving Words

REFERRING TO Emily Dickinson in a recent NY Times article, Holland Carter wrote, "The one power (she) trusted was the power of language, which she loved. ... By her own account she experienced **an acute physical reaction to words, a euphoric shock.**"

How would she react, I wonder, to recent developments? I'm thinking of the legions of word lovers one hundred and fifty years later writing and reading columns like this one ... and Blogs like Mark Peters' **"Wordlustitude"** where he recently posted his word- of-the-day, **"nanoblahblah"** defined as **"a tiny bit of nonsense" i.e., "small talk."** Cited usage: "If your pillow talk is limited to **nanoblahblah**, your partner may not be around for long!"

It may sound silly, but it's very clever. **Nano-** from ancient Greek, **nanos/dwarf**, and **blah/silly chatter**, which entered our dictionaries in 1918, are combined by a self-styled lexicographer who, in his contemporary way, is every bit as smitten by the look and sound of words as Emily was. (Had Mark been in Amherst in the late 1850's, they might have been soul mates!)

Nano- was also chosen in 1959 to combine with the 14th century **second** to define a newly conceived time unit, **one billionth of a second.**

John Ciardi, in the Foreword to his brilliant **"Browser's Dictionary,"** writes, "Linnaeus would have done better to call us *Homo loquens,* 'speaking man.' For though our racial sapience remains in doubt, our loquacity is beyond question ... Man is the animal that uses language."

He continues, "Lewis Thomas in his 'Lives of a Cell' describes the nonstop and precision labor of an anthill, ... asks if there is any similar ceaseless activity of humankind, and answers that ... **it is the endless making, multiplying, and changing of language."**

John Tierney in his May 18 NYT column, "Doomsayers Beware, A Bright Future Beckons," writes, "Progress this century could be impeded by politics, wars, plagues or climate change, but Dr. Ridley argues (in his new book, "The Rational Optimist") that, as usual, the **"apocoholics"** are overstating the risks and underestimating innovative responses." The word is a fun play on the words, **apocalypse and alcoholic**, creating **"those addicted to apocalypse theories"** ... a new word that could catch on.

ABC News reported recently on **"narco-terrorists"** operating around the border areas between the US and Mexico. While it's not yet in the dictionary, we know exactly what it means, thanks to the words-savvy person who joined two ideas.

Ross Douthat in a recent NYT column, "Europe's Minaret Moment" used the word **"dhimmitude,"** coined in Lebanon in 1982 to mean **"producing a state of servility to an Islamic majority."** It's derived **from an old Arabic word dhimma/Islamic Sharia or laws.** Douthat writes,

"... envisioning a Muslim-majority 'Eurabia,' ... the most likely scenario for Europe isn't **dhimmitude;** it's a long period of tension, punctuated by spasms of violence, that makes the continent a more unpleasant place without fundamentally transforming it."

In this age of globalization and flash-fast transportation of goods and ideas, **our words will come from all over the planet,** marrying up, shot-gun style, with words from different cultures to define new concepts.

I'm euphoric!

A "Kist of Ferlies"
In Key West

A **"KIST OF FERLIES"** was the rapturous term used by Douglas Young to describe (John) "Jamieson's Dictionary of Scots" when it was first published in 1808. It translates as **"a treasure trove of wonders."**

Here are a few of those wonders from the 2008 e-publication of that iconic work:

Todle ... the murmuring noise caused by meat boiling
 gently in a pot
Fair bumbazed ... really confused
Perjink ... precise, finicky

Contemporary critics agree "Jamieson had an ear for the marvellous, but he also relished the ordinary..."

Now I want to rapturize in similar fashion over Nadja Hansen, Associate Editor, *Solares Hill* (Sunday supplement to *The Key West Citizen*), and her "overline," a different phrase that floats, without context, reference, or attribution, above the masthead each week. If you were to collect these, as I do, you would soon realize that she is a lexical wonder. She pooh-poohs the notion, shrugging off my insistence that they are precious, provocative nuggets with a smile, and, "I'm so glad you like them."

To begin to appreciate them, imagine you are seeing *Solares Hill* for the first time, and as your eyes scan the front page you spy this at the very top:

Quondam Quixotic Quidnunc Quits

How do you react? You might feel disoriented and ask yourself questions. What does it mean? Why is it there? What does it refer to? What should you do with it? There is no asterisk, nothing that tells you. There is no explicit challenge thrown down. It is not like anything you have ever experienced in reading a newspaper. You might smile at it, but then ignore it for the sake of preserving your mental comfort. OR, you might open your mind, accept its presence, and sense that, whatever it's supposed to be, it fits well with the unconventional, literary *Solares Hill* in particular, and Key West in general.

It took me a while, but I soon realized how I looked forward to the next Sunday's nugget. Then I called *Solares Hill* Editor, Mark Howell, discovered they were her creation, and invited myself to meet Nadja and learn more.

They pop into her mind, she says, while reading, checking words in the dictionary, playing Scrabble online, doing Crosswords, or as aural or visual relatives of words she comes across in the course of a day's work. She likes to share them, but resists telling readers what to make of them. "Each person will react differently," she says in a gentle understatement. And that, of course, is the beauty of them... they are yours to do with as you will, as they were hers to create without rules, restrictions, or formula.

For me, they are a good excuse to haul out my *American Heritage Dictionary*. Let's look at a few of Nadja's nuggets from recent issues:

A Peculiar Peccavi
Clerisy Writing Clerihews
Mystifying Creative Maieutics
Fossicking in the Wadis

Each contains at least one word that might send you to the dictionary, along with a few others, which, together, make a fine bit of nonsense/knowledge.

She plays with puns and poetry...

May the Horse be with Hue
Linnets Playing in the Misty Linns
Dark Horses of Another Color
Chameleons Chasing Rainbows

Onomatopoeia, alliteration, whimsy, polysemy, and homophony all find a berth in her oeuvre...

Cockahoop Cockalorum
Jilted, Jolted Janissary
Wearing a Kaross in the Karroo
By Comparison, the Carapace is no Caparison

Nadja's personal favorite is a mash-up of word play and sensitivity to life...

Fish Crying in Their Soup.

In his 1952 *Language As Gesture* (Columbia University Press), R.P. Blackmur, writing on Wallace Stevens' poem, "The Ordinary Women," focuses on one atmospheric stanza...

The lacquered loges huddled there
Mumbled zay-zay and a-zay, a-zay.
The moonlight
Fubbed the girandoles

...and comments, "The strange phrase, **"fubbed the girandoles" ("cheated the chandeliers" in that the moonlight was stronger than the artificial light),** has an inexplicable charm: the approach of language, through the magic of elegance, to nonsense. That the phrase is not nonsense, that on inspection it retrieves itself to sense, is its inner virtue. Somewhere between the realms of ornamental sound and representative statement, the words pause and balance, dissolve and resolve."

I think that is a good analysis of **"Nadja's Nuggets"** as well.

Of course, they all translate as **"Crazy About Words."**

Silent Knights

I THINK we must all have our **words-with-silent-letters** stories, recollections of how we've embarrassed ourselves, laughed at ourselves, screamed at ourselves, for our gaffes.

To test this theory, I decided last week to ask the next person I encountered. Immediately, he recalled a situation many years ago when, in conversation with a small group at a college reunion, he used the word **subtle**...blithely pronouncing the *b*. He remembers the silence, followed by the laughter, followed by the lifelong reminder every time he sees or hears the word.

So, I realized, my **raspberry** story is not a personal fixation... I can share it. I was one of the last two standing in a seventh grade spelling bee. But when I left out the *p,* and "Miss Smarty Pants," Lauranna Banks, put it in, I had failed to win a spelling bee for the first time.

Reading recently of the 9 Muses in Greek mythology, I discovered that their parents are Zeus and **Mnemosyne**, the Goddess of Memory, (she of **mnemonic device** fame). The irony of the truth that I never say **mnemonic device** aloud, because I can never remember if it's the **m** or the **n** that's silent, helped me make up my mind to write about these **devil-silent-letter-words.**

Why? we ask. Why not phoneticise **de(b)t, i(s)land, dam(n), (h)onest, & ans(w)er,** as is being done by linguists developing alphabets for previously unwritten languages, and in new planned languages like Interlingua and Esperanto? Or, at least, use **"Ø" which symbolizes zero sound,** after mute letters, as has been proposed by less radical change proponents?

Well, if you think **Y2K** was a big deal, can you imagine the chaos and mayhem surrounding such a switch? Every **knight would have his shield,** and look like this: **kØnight,** and the poor **knish** would be screaming, "Don't give *me* one of those things... **I'm not a nish!"**

And can you hear the ongoing debates with the language purists who pride themselves on knowing that ***ps-*** beginnings, as in **psychology** and **pseudonym,** and the initial ***mn*** as in **mnemonics,** originated in the Greek, from which we derive so many of our beautiful words? ... and that spurious letters, **like the *b* in debt & doubt** were purposelyly inserted at some point to reference Latin **cognates** like **debit & dubitable**? ... and that, over the centuries, many pronunciation changes have occurred without spelling changes, e.g., the ***-th* in asthma and the *t* in Christmas became silent in spoken** English? ... and that the **digraph "gh" was pronounced "x" in Old English words** such as **light!?**

And so many words have come directly into our language from French, which is a heaven full of silent letters. To this day I have to think twice before I order **prix-fixe** from a menu.

There is something poetic, magical, and very special in all that etymology despite the irritability it sometimes causes. We cherish many impractical things in this world, and sometimes use them in very effective ways. I am the proud owner of a 3x4 piece of canvas, which I purchased at a yard sale in the '80s for a dime; it has metal grommets on the corners and must have been used as an outdoor ad in the '50s or '60s. Over a sketch of 4 young people dressed in jeans, it reads, "**Wremember the "w" is silent. WRANGLER, the wreal sportswear**"... priceless!

Owning that canvas finally inspired me to look up **raspberry** and to discover that it was named for **raspis**, an Old English sweet wine distilled from the **raspberry**.

So, *that's* **why!**

May I Borrow A Word Or Two?

THE YEAR 1066 was a great one for our language if not for the Anglo-Saxon people of the British Isles. William the Conqueror might have delivered a variation on Julius Caesar's "Mission Accomplished," his "veni, vidi, vici," with "We came (across the channel), we spoke (our more genteel words), we conquered (the grunty sound of your native tongue)."

Within a few hundred years, English was transformed. Old English (OE in your dictionary) yielded to the much simpler grammar and the enriched vocabulary of Middle English (ME). **Our language had successfully adapted under the direst circumstances: invasion and subjugation. Fully one third of its words were now Anglicized French.** This was a good thing for two reasons: 1) they were "civilizing" words, i.e., words of jurisprudence and governance, and of ranks of aristocracy, which reflected the beginnings of a departure from serfdom, and 2) they established the English language as a **"borrowing tongue."** (I highly recommend Bill Bryson's "The Mother Tongue: English and How It Got That Way," for an in-depth but delightful and easy to read history.)

The words introduced into English following the Norman Conquest are so embedded that we barely sense they are from Old French (OF) unless we notice the etymological info in brackets before the definitions of words like *beautiful, justice, marriage, baron, parliament, prison & petty.*

Those that came later, in the modern English period (mod.), roughly beginning in Shakespeare's time, and up to the present, reflect the continued expansion and diversity of thought and interest of the English speaking peoples. (Let's face it, we had continent-envy. Civilization moved from East to West.) These words and expressions are far more easily identifiable as French. In many cases, they have simply transferred "as is." In this category are *avant-garde, repartee, bon vivant, demi tasse, coup d'etat, encore, joie de vivre, objet d'art, double entendre, protégé,* and thousands more.

In the twenty-first century, about one third of the words we use most are from French.

And I've heard it said, "an English speaking person preparing to study French today doesn't realize that he already knows more than 15,000 words!" **The spelling and pronunciation may differ significantly, as in jeter/to throw (jettison), pendre/to hang (pending), & repondre/to reply (respond),** but awareness of the historic relationship of the two languages helps the novice gain facility in French.

Bryson writes, "… the language we speak today is rich and expressive not so much because new words were imposed on it as because they were *welcomed*."

The wave of interest in Eastern philosophy has brought us **yoga, namaste, prana, and ohm.** And many of us, feeling too rushed, yearn for more of a

manana mentality; **"tomorrow"** just doesn't work as well.

These are a few examples of words English has borrowed from 146 "other" languages. Most languages are simply not "foreign" to us!

Although we are generally welcoming, our society still has its share of cultural and language-grunts. Recently I encountered a man who would not say, no less taste, **quiche.** He referred to the rest of us at a Deli that was featuring it as "you people and your **quickies**!"

C'est la vie!

Words as Madeleines

IN HIS Chandleresque novel, "Gun With Occasional Music," Jonathan Lethem's protagonist says, "I don't possess an **eidetic (photographic)** memory, but I had a picture of her knees – and the creamy inches of skin above them – burned into my consciousness from the brief flash as I walked in."

We all know how the senses can bring back memories. Sniff an aroma in the air, and you're in a time warp. I grew up about a mile from the Silvercup bread factory in Long Island City. To this day the smell of freshly baked white bread... I can feel it now, sticking to the roof of my mouth like peanut butter! So the strains of a melody, or the look of sawdust on a floor, can unlock memories that are associated with these sensory experiences. One of the great literary references to sensory-prompted memory is made in Marcel Proust's *Remembrance of Things Past* where he becomes aware that the taste of a **madeleine... a small sweet sponge cake** can trigger very detailed and pleasant memories.

Earlier this year, while enrolled in a six-week memoir-writing workshop, I found that **words triggered memories** for me too.

E.g., the word **lanky** in a NYT review describing a dancer, brought me back in front of my high school track coach, who used the word to explain why, low to the ground as I am, I could never be a great cross-country runner. I remembered the feeling as though it were yesterday, and was able to write about how I proved him wrong.

Similarly, the word **bungalow,** which I hadn't heard in a long time, served as a flashlight in the dark cave of my memory. Happily remembered stories from childhood summers at my grandfather's bungalow in Rocky Point came back to me.

What words trigger memories for you?

Just for fun, I imagined, from a list in Simon Hertnon's wonderful **"Endangered Words"** (Skyhorse, 2009), a few that might make some famous people nostalgic. Mark Twain who said, " Do not put off till tomorrow what can be put off till day-after-tomorrow..." might like **perendinate,** which means precisely that, whereas **procrastinate,** technically refers to a delay only until tomorrow. They are, however, used synonymously.

Chavish (the mingled din of many birds) might bring back memories for Tippi Hedren, the star of Hitchcock's "The Birds." In the movie, she was driven daffy by the sound of it.

Noah's adventures might be instantly recalled on his hearing the word **pluviose (rainy).** Hertnon selected it because he liked its potential poetic and figurative use, e.g., pluviose tears. He suggests it has a superlative connotation as well, which lends to its appeal.

And he feels that **offing (at a distance from the shore)** "is a little gem worth rescuing." It is used mostly in the idiom, "in the offing," to mean nearby, in the sense of time or distance; e.g., "a waiter hovered in the offing." I had fun picturing those Caribe Indians looking out to sea saying, "Nina, Pinta, and Santa Maria... lifestyle change in the offing!"

Finally, if she heard the word **sicko (*slang*, 1975, meaning deranged),** Virginia Woolf might remember the day she wrote a 181-word opening sentence to her essay, "On Being Ill." Some critics feel it is the most perfect sentence ever written.

I'll quote it here sometime so no one accuses *me* of running on!

Welcome, <u>Queen Elizabeth,</u> <u>To "Crazy About Words"</u>

WITH DICTIONARY held high, the Queen joined our circle of word lovers with a triumphant declaration. In Alan Bennett's marvelous novella, *The Uncommon Reader,* she exclaims, "I've discovered what I am. I am an **opsimath." (one who begins to study and learn late in life...** from Greek, opse--late, and math--learn.)

In a richly imagined and hilarious paean to reading, Bennett has her become a viral reader, to the consternation of the government, the palace, and her family. This little gem of a book is guaranteed to delight readers as it did my class, "Reading Like A Writer," last Fall. That was soon after the Queen herself blurred the line between reality and fiction when she "parachuted" into the opening ceremonies of the 2012 Olympic Games with the help of James Bond.

Among its pleasures, are a slew of words, phrases, and pure Britishisms Bennett employs to enrich his prose.

At a State dinner in the opening scene, the Queen asks the President of France about the writer Jean Genet. "Unbriefed on the **glabrous** playwright and novelist, the president looked wildly about for his minister of culture."

(glabrous...smooth skinned; free from hair or down; used to describe skin or a leaf.)

While her interest in reading was still nascent, Bennett writes, "Had Her Majesty gone for another **duff** read, an early George Eliot, say, or a late Henry James, novice reader that she was, she might have been put off reading for good and there would be no story to tell." **Duff** is a noun of uncertain origin applied to **decaying vegetable matter covering the ground under trees,** then later to other forms of **rubbish**; hence, as an adjective, and in the sense here, **anything worthless.** In another sense, probably derived from **dough**, the word means **a flour pudding, boiled or steamed in a cloth** (picture it!); it's only a bit of a stretch of the imagination to see how it came to be applied to **the buttocks.**

The Queen's private secretary, Sir Kevin, a Kiwi with whom she will do battle over her reading, had, when he was appointed, "been hailed in the press as a new broom, a young(ish) man who would sweep away some of the redundant deference and more flagrant **flummeries** that were monarchy's customary accretions..." **... empty compliments, nonsense.** The word also means **a sweet dish made with beaten eggs, sugar, and flavorings**; in this sense, it dates to 17th century Wales, and the word **llymru** meaning **soft, slippery...** just like idle compliments! (The etymologies of many English words seem to lead us to boiled puddings!)

In the democratic and generous spirit of this story, the Queen at one point says to Norman, who had been instrumental in getting her into reading, "I know the word for you ... you change my library books, you look up awkward words in the dictionary and find me the quotations. Do you know what you are?"

"I used to be a **skivvy**, ma'am."

"Well, you're not a **skivvy** now. You're my **amanuensis**." Norman looked it up in the dictionary the Queen now kept always on her desk. "... **a literary assistant.**"

In Britain, a **skivvy** is a **low paid domestic.** (Norman had worked in the kitchens before the Queen brought him up.) In America, the word is best known as **underwear,** originated in the US Navy.

In a verbal joust, Sir Kevin says to the Queen, "To read is to withdraw. To make oneself unavailable. One would feel easier about it," said Sir Kevin, "if the pursuit were less ... selfish."

"Selfish?" queries the Queen.

"Perhaps I should say **solipsistic.**"

"Perhaps you should." **(of the view that the self is all that can be known to exist...as opposed to denying others something out of greed.)**

Toward the end of the novella, as the Queen asserts herself in her new persona, we read, "... within days Gerald was no longer in attendance on Her Majesty and indeed no longer in the household at all, but back with his scarcely remembered regiment **yomping** in the rain over the moors of Northumberland. The speed of his almost Tudor dispatch..." **(yomping...marching with heavy equipment over difficult terrain...** origin unknown and only dates to the 1980s).

There's a wonderful description of the family's reaction to the Queen's new passion. Had it been her responsibility to "dust and hoover the house," Bennett teases us, standards might have fallen, but of course that was not the case. "She had always kept them up to the mark and age had not made her more indulgent. (But) reading (as she was), ... she left the family more to themselves, **chivvied (vexed or harassed)** them hardly at all, and they had an easier time all round." Originally a Scottish noun denoting a **hunting cry**, it later came to be a verb meaning **to chase, to worry.**

My favorite expression in the entire novella, which makes me chuckle whenever I think of it, comes up when the Queen "embarks on a new conversational gambit."

"What are you reading at the moment?" she might ask. With the result that "a growing number of her loving subjects ... regretting that they had not performed well and feeling, too, that the monarch had somehow **bowled them a googly**." **(to surprise them, to throw them for a loop...** a term adapted from cricket).

If you appreciate excellent storytelling and sharp dialogue (Bennett is the playwright who gave us *The History Boys* and *The Madness of George III*), if you enjoy laughing out loud, and if you want to discover a perfect $10 gift item, get yourself a copy of *The Uncommon Reader*. If I've given away too much of the plot while sharing some of his words, it doesn't matter. You'll be reading it over and over anyway.

Dictionary Mania

RALPH WALDO EMERSON said, **"Every word was once a poem."** It's an etymologist's delight, reminding us that every word, like a poem, originated from one someone's necessity to express a thought. Like **'emoticon,' (1994), a word blend of 'emotion' and 'icon,' meaning a symbol, like a smiley face ☺, used in email.**

I recall Emerson's quote each year at this time as my "Crazy About Words" volunteers and I personalize and distribute copies of

A Student's Dictionary to over 300 Third Graders at nine schools here on the East End of Long Island, as local sponsors of **"The Dictionary Project"***

"Adopt a pet letter..." I urge the kids, after they've each been called up by name, in a gathering in the school cafeteria, auditorium, or, if it's recent construction, the **cafeterium**. "Now find the section in your dictionary devoted to that letter..."

I don't believe any fabulous dignitary invited to speak and distribute diplomas at an Ivy League graduation could feel better than we do watching a gaggle of 8-9 year old boys and girls peek into a personalized copy of their very own first dictionary. The wriggling and giggling and sharing of discoveries as they flip the pages would give heart to anyone worried about the future of print.

"Next, look for a 5-letter word you don't know, beginning with that letter," I guide them. This, I believe, was what Emerson had in mind; the *discovery* of a word too, is poetry!

Let's play an adult version of this game. Wherever you, dear "Crazy About Words" reader, are sitting at this moment, reach for your favorite dictionary and open it to a random page...

I've flipped open to p. 311 of my *Webster's College Dictionary*, a page full of words with **"counter-"** as prefix. I run my finger down the left column, and discover **'counterpane'...a quilt.** But the formation isn't clear to me until I look up **'pane'** as well. It's from Latin **pannus ... cloth or rag.** Along the etymological path, it became, specifically, a *small* square of cloth (and then extended to a small square of glass in a frame, a sheet of postage stamps, etc.) Together with **'counter-'...contrasting, opposing**, it nicely describes the selection of clashing colors and/or designs that typify **quilt** patterns.

Not surprisingly, I jump on **'counterword'** in the right column of the same page. It means a word that **originally had a specific meaning, but now is used in a general sense, like 'swell'** (originally meant 'stylish'). **'Awful'** ('afraid') **& 'terrific'** ('terrifying') are also examples of **'counterwords.'**

I flip again and find myself on the first page of "I"... I've never seen **'iatrogenic'** before, from **Greek 'iatros' ... physician.** The word came into our borrow-like-crazy language in 1924, perhaps in connection with an early medical malpractice case. It means **'induced inadvertently by a physician or his treatment.'**

A baby flip brings me to a "J" page and I see that **'just'** has fifteen distinct meanings, seven as an adverb, and eight as an adjective. All come down to us **from the Latin 'jus'... law/right**... a little word just full of energy and ambition!

Next, I land on **'plafond'** (the 'd' is silent); it came into English from across the Channel around 1650, along with the decorating style, to describe **a ceiling, flat or arched, and highly decorated or painted, such as is seen in churches and palace staterooms.** It must have all started with Michelangelo a century earlier!

Another flip, and I learn that **'settee' (1710 a.d.) ... a seat for two or more** is a variation of **'settle' (900 a.d.) ... a high backed wooden bench.**

This entire 'game' of "Dictionary Mania" took about fifteen minutes, and satisfied my word lust for the time being. I'm not about to follow in the footsteps of Ammon Shea, author of *Reading the OED: One Man, One Year, 21,730 Pages*. That has no appeal for me. But flipping through my favorite dictionary once in a while: PRICELESS!

By the way, the kids' hottest discoveries were **"knave," "cache," "dally" and "hovel"** ... pure poetry for them!

*"The Dictionary Project" is a non-profit which has, since 1995, distributed over 17,000,000 dictionaries, through local sponsors, to third graders throughout the US. As of 2012, 52% of US schools are covered. Check out their Website for more information, and to see what opportunities you have to participate in this amazing literacy project. www.dictionaryproject.org

The Invigilators

MOST OF US can remember them, though we may not have known they were called anything but **"exam monitors**." **Invigilators** had the tough job of appearing watchful every time you looked up from your paper, wondering, with eyes rolling, what the heck a particular test question meant. The word dates to the 16th century in English, **from the Latin, "watched over,"** and is defined as **"one who supervises candidates during an examination."** (Although "Premium Rush," a new action-thriller about *bicycle messengers,* of all things, has been well reviewed, I think we can safely bet against anyone producing a movie with the same subject or title as this month's column anytime soon!)

"Learning Words" is our subject, in celebration of Back-to-School time and of the 10th anniversary of the Lifetime Learning Program at Peconic Landing where I write and teach. Our learning activities, as we puzzle our way through life, have generated a vocabulary owing much to Greek roots.

Words like **pedagogue** (child-leading) and its lesser known companion, **andragogue** (adult-leading) are classic, and contrast different styles of teaching. Once they've done their kid-drills with a pedagogue in an **abecedarian** environment, children, like adults, learn best with an andragogue in a **progressive learning** environment. Thus, the word **andragogy** came to apply to the theory of **"adult education"** in which learners drive the process with their questions/desire to learn, while teachers facilitate. John Dewey developed his theories of progressive learning in the first half of the 20th century, and Malcolm Knowles championed adult education and the idea of lifelong learning in the latter half.

Autodidacts, self-taught persons who learn outside of an educational institution, are fascinating creatures who have the self-discipline to study and/or practice on their own to master a skill or increase their understanding of a particular subject. Whether achieved with or without a teacher, a **polymath** is **learned in many diverse subjects**, and is most often referred to as **a renaissance (wo)man**.

"Brainstorming" produces ideas in a collaborative, non-judgmental environment, "putting our heads together," we might say. The term was coined by Alex Osborn, the "O" of BBD&O advertising agency, in the 1940s, to describe a process in which minds feed off one another for their mutual learning benefit. The term is now also applied to a singular effort to bring all of one's wits to bear on a problem...so it is no longer oxymoronic to brainstorm on your own. And, **"crowdsourcing"** is a hot new word meaning **to solicit ideas from a large group** with something in common, kind of like the old-fashioned **survey.**

In education, the **"pygmalion effect"** describes **a phenomenon in which a student does well or poorly depending on the expectations of others, including teachers.** "We expect big things of you," communicated to a student in various ways, leads to positive performance, and vice versa. The term comes from George Bernard Shaw's "Pygmalion," later the musical, "My Fair Lady," lampooning the British class system. Eliza Doolittle, a Cockney flower girl, was taught to speak "properly" by Professor Henry Higgins, and convinced herself that she was a lady.

The class **dunce**, by contrast, remains **unable to learn anything** as long as the teacher keeps giving him that awful **eponymous** label. **Named after** John Duns Scotus, a 17th century philosopher, whose followers were referred to derisively as "Dunsmen" by those who disagreed with his theories, the unenlightened term (and the pointed cap) found its way into the vocabulary of childhood education and has been used until fairly recently.

For all the academic and experiential ways children and adults learn, it's only in the **"aha! moments"** when individuals **realize** something or embrace information that becomes part of who they are. I once heard a speaker say that this word should be spelled **"real-eyes"** to better express how distinct such learning is from all the stuff we learn simply to pass tests.

We are cradle-to-grave learners, all of us. When we **real-eyes** this, we may become more aware too of how **open-minded** we might be to fresh ideas and new information.

I hope these "learning words" will help you negotiate the learning process, whatever your age. Happy learning!

Spring Collection

WE WAKE these April mornings to **"sparrowy air,"** as the poet, Richard Wilbur, so richly put it. Step out early, exult in the bird sounds, and you'll understand how elegant and apt a phrase that is. It's doubtful anyone has used it before, as "sparrowy" is not a *proper* adjective. It's simply a great example of our language manipulated to serve as poet's paint.

I enjoy the first color that comes to the woods, the white blossoms of the **shadblow** bush, on my daily walks here on Eastern Long Island. When all is yet monochromatic in the woods, they appear as cotton balls suspended over **vernal ponds**, those seasonal wet spots that look like big mucky inkwells and provide spawning ground for wood frogs at this time of year. Later in the season, the shadblow bear sweet purplish-black berries called **Juneberries or Serviceberries** that Meriwether Lewis wrote, in 1805, saved his expedition from starvation. He must have been in competition with the local Indians who prized the fruit, and the bluebirds too.

I hadn't heard of a **drumlin (an elongated, tapered hill formed by glacial ice acting on the ground moraine)** before I read of Don Paterson, a star Scottish poet, who traveled one Spring to Luing, a tiny obscure island in the Hebrides, in search of "intimate exile." The sign that greeted him on his arrival by ferry assured him he'd come to the right place: *Welcome to our*

Island/ A place to think...a place to be. He describes it as a walker's utopia and climbed its centrally located **drumlin**, clearly distinct on the landscape, several times. His success in regenerating himself is described in two lines of his poem, "Luing" ... *Here, beside the fordable Atlantic/...the* **fontanelles** *reopen one by one.* **Fontanelles ... the soft spots on a baby's head where the skull hasn't yet fully fused.**

The exotic **samizdat** comes up in connection with the Arab Spring and Occupy Wall Street movements. It's a Russian word meaning **self-published**, and refers to **protest literature**, usually produced or copied by hand and not professional looking. It was first used in the Soviet Union where documents and treatises were illegally hand copied and passed from person to person in secret. Can't you just picture some angry Vladimir spitting out the word venomously as he seizes a piece of **samizdat** from a downtrodden worker!

Fifteen years ago this spelling bee season, Rebecca Sealfon made history with her YouTube-worthy, winning response to spell **E-U-O-N-Y-M.** (If you'd like to see it, just Google the word. It's only 38 precious seconds long!) It's from the Greek, **eu ... good** and **onym ... name**, and means **an appropriately named person, place, or thing.** E.g., Rex Pound is a euonym for a Dog Catcher! Despite its classic root, it only goes back to 1889 in English, when, inspired by Lewis Carroll and other crazies, playing with words became very fashionable. The adjective form is **euonymous**, not to be confused with the shrub cultivated for its decorative foliage or fruit, named

euonymus, pronounced alike and derived from the same root.

As roots like horseradish are Spring comestibles, and as Frank Bruni, formerly fat food writer, (see his wonderful memoir, "Born Round") used **ipecac** in his NYT OpEd recently, I'm considering the word legit for this Spring collection. **Ipecac** is a Brazilian shrub whose roots and rhizomes are used to make **ipecac syrup**, an **emetic** widely used in the last century as an antidote to food poisoning. Bruni used it in describing Rick Santorum's reaction ("I felt like throwing up") to JFK's talk on separation of church and state, "He outdid himself...by casting Camelot as **ipecac** ..." The word is a shortened spelling of the Portuguese name for the plant, **ipecacuanha**, which comes from the Tupi, spoken by ethnic tribes along the coast of Brazil.

Happy Spring!

<u>Lanky</u>

THAT WORD **"lanky"** came up again recently. The NY Times, writing of Savion Glover, the dancer/choreographer, proclaimed, "strength doesn't stop at his feet, ... It pumps through his body, *lanky* and tightly wound, radiating out like an electrical force."

I felt a familiar pang, though it's been many years since Bill Miles, my high school track coach, used the word in answering my question. "What can I do to qualify for the varsity cross-country Team?" I'd asked. I was a junior that year, with a decent record and a few medals on the one-and-a-quarter-mile freshman course, and on the two-and-a-half-mile course we began running as sophomores. But I was still "JV"--Junior Varsity-- desperate for my varsity letter, the girl magnet. It was the fifties.

"You're not *lanky* enough to be a really good cross-country runner, Mc Kay," he answered. "Look at Beyer, and Baxter, and Cawley; their stride is so nice and long. They eat up ground in a way runners with shorter legs, like you, just can't do. And that's what makes the one-to-two minute difference for the course between your times and theirs."

I did look. And for the first time, I appreciated how their strides seemed gazelle-like as they crossed "the flats" and the other level parts of the course. Then I looked at the tag in Pete Beyer's trousers hanging in the locker room:

26x33. His legs were four inches longer than mine. I thought about this and did the math.

Running against Pete, I'd either have to take seven strides for his six over the whole course just to keep even, or I'd drop behind him at the rate of about twenty-five yards every minute, which was basically what was happening. So most Saturdays at Van Cortland Park in The Bronx, where the meets were held, he took home a varsity medal, while I sometimes won a JV medal. There was no comfort in the math.

Physics turned out to be a different story. The conventional wisdom in cross-country running was that going uphill, a good runner simply tries to maintain his pace. "Don't try to make time in the hills," was the way Coach Miles put it. But after the way he answered my question, I realized he was speaking to his ideal lanky runners. As for a runner with my physique, maybe that wasn't the best advice.

I might not be **lanky**, but I'm not squatty either; it was not a Sisyphian task for me to get myself up a hill. As a matter of fact, I noticed that my body's natural inclination was to crouch low a bit as I started up a hill and to run faster, pumping my arms. So I tried it out during weekday practices in Prospect Park in Brooklyn, where we ran every Monday through Thursday. What an eye-opener it was!

"Whadda ya doin' Mc Kay?" gasped Cawley as I passed him. "Just experimenting," I called over my shoulder as I mounted the top of a hill and flew down the other side without braking. I tried it again on the next hill and found my lungs had more capacity than I'd realized, equal to the challenge of gaining time and passing other runners where it was not recommended to do so. I was exhilarated. I practiced that way all week, and it felt natural for me.

The next Saturday, a beautiful mid-October day, was the "Manhattan Invitational," the third major meet of the season. "Bang"! sounded the starter's gun as the butterflies yielded to a full-body focus on the "cow path," the narrow entrance to the hills a half mile away across a wide plain called "the flats." "Like thunder" is the only way to describe the sound of seven hundred runners funneling to be in the front rank because "you don't make time in the hills." As usual, the "lankies" got there first, but I had confidence in the radical style I'd developed in the past week, and I couldn't wait to give it a try now.

The trail, as it entered the "cow path" was only about eight or nine feet wide, so what had been seven hundred boys abreast at the starting line three minutes earlier was now pretty much a single file... with room for passing, of course. At this point, I judged that there were maybe thirty guys ahead of me. I settled in after the half-mile sprint, enjoying the sense of my body moving quite effortlessly through the cool dry air, then began to judge the steepness and length of each hill as I approached it.

By crouching just a bit, leaning into the hill, and shortening my steps, I found it comfortable to speed up and pass one runner after another. It worked as well on "Cemetery Hill," past the burial ground of the Van Cortland family, which everyone thought was aptly named because it was such a killer. The effect was like riding an escalator running parallel to people walking the stairs. I kept going ... doing the same thing on hill after hill ... amazed at the simple physical principle underlying my new found prowess. I felt I was using my body and lungs to their best advantage.

The course concludes, after a mile and a half in the hills, with another flat half mile on a narrow track along the base of a high stone cliff to the finish line. I let go and flew down the last steep hill, hoping the lack of control at such speed would not trip me up. As I turned into the flat section I looked up and saw that there was no one in front of me. In another three minutes or so, I breasted the first finish ribbon of my life. I had won the JV gold medal!

Coach Miles at the finish line was visibly shocked to see me coming down the home stretch in first place. A while later, he asked how I'd done it, and I told him the story as I've recorded it here. He smiled, and told me I'd have a place on the varsity team the following week. But he never commented on my strategy, almost as though it was too alien to talk about. While I would like to have been credited for my ingenuity and imagined that other un-lanky runners could benefit from using the simple trick I'd learned, I soon realized that it was to my advantage to keep it to myself.

I continued to surprise runners in the hills for the rest of my high school cross-country days. I won 24 more medals--gold, bronze and silver--in my junior and senior years. And I gave my varsity letter, sewn over the pocket of a sweater that was miles too big for her, to Eileen Kelly.

To this day, when I'm out for a hike and approach a modest Long Island hill, my body remembers the technique I developed for my unlanky body, and responds.

Have Fun With Your Dictionary

AN ITEM in the *NYTimes* caught my word-roving eye. Reporting on the pride the Dutch felt over the 400th anniversary celebrations of New Amsterdam, it included a photo captioned, "a girl tries on traditional Dutch clogs called ***klompen***."

What a perfect ***onomatopoeic*** word, I thought. Verlyn Klinkenborg, in his *NYTimes* essay, "How The Thunder Sounds," wrote "Onomatopoeia is such a delicate thing." But, in this case, ***klompen*** seems to mimic the ***klomp-klomp*** sound those wooden shoes make on any surface but grass. I looked up ***klomp*** in the dictionary, as it is used by writers occasionally describing the sound of high heeled or boot clad feet moving across a wooden floor.

No luck, because in English it's properly spelled **clomp.** But my reward for looking was finding the only word in the English language beginning with "klo." ***Kloof***, is a word from Afrikaans meaning, ***a deep glen, ravine.*** Although it must be related to "cliff," there was no reference to such a connection. But, again, a reward for my research effort: I found the adjective, ***cliffy***, which will surely come in handy to describe some landscapes or Evel Knevel's motorcycle leaps.

Am I making a good case for looking up "stuff" in the dictionary, just for fun and to kindle your imagination? Well, listen to this beauty! Watching a famous person's funeral on TV, I was prompted to check out the precise definition of **basilica**, how it's different from a church. It's *the name given to certain churches granted special privileges by the pope.* Not particularly memorable, but I'll never forget **basilisk** just below it on my dictionary page, *a legendary reptile with fatal breath and glance.*

Now there's an image I've got to get some child to draw for me, because my own inner-child is far too inhibited to imagine it in all its glorious detail. Most of us have a loved one or dog in our lives who has "bad breath," but "fatal breath *and* glance" … Wow! I must remember to give that one to my nephew who beautifully described the cartoon character, Dudley Dooright, as having "an outrageously heroic chin."

Do go to the dictionary at the slightest provocation, and while you're on the page with the word that got you there, let your eyes wander and find at least one interesting bonus word for your trouble.

I got to musing recently about a **polka dot**. Is the phrase derived from the Bohemian dance that we know? (No indication of that in my dictionary.) And, is there such a thing as one **polka dot?** Or is it just a plain old ordinary dot until joined by others in a field of them? It's kind of a philosophical question, don't you think? I mean, how can a dot lose its identity simply because you remove others from around it? Even if you were the last person on earth, you'd still be you, wouldn't you? Lonely, perhaps, but still you.

My dictionary, being an objective friend, insisted that it had to be part of a pattern to be a ***polka dot***. And I discovered that ***Polka*** is also ***a female Polish person, (Polack, the male).*** Now I can say I've seen many a polka-dotted Polka doing the polka!

Oh, my!

Et cetera, et cetera, et cetera

WHO KNEW little old **"etc."** came from such a long and noble lexical line? Not I. I've taken it for granted all my life, tossing it in at the end of lists in sentences, as though to say, "you know the rest," or "you get the idea."

My interest was piqued recently when I saw the 1946 film, "Anna and the King of Siam," starring Rex Harrison and Irene Dunn, on TCM. Harrison, as the King in the 1860s , is working hard to learn English, the better to lead his country into modernity, and he likes to show off his linguistic prowess. At the end of many spoken sentences, he enunciates each syllable of **"et cetera, et cetera, et cetera"** with such a flourish of his hands and an almost beatific grin that I began to suspect there must be a good backstory.

So I did what any red-blooded, English-speaking logophile would do… I Googled **"et cetera."** Sure enough, its use is legendary among monarchs who wanted to demonstrate their knowledge of many things along with their importance in not having to list them in detail.

Going back to Roman times, it was especially useful to a Caesar who did not have to repeatedly list all the accumulated territorial dynastic claims that followed his eminence's name and title. Fast forward and hear a Tsar proclaiming, "We, Nicholas II of Russia, By the Grace of God, Emperor and Autocrat of All the Russias, King of

Poland, Grand Duke of Finland, **et cetera, et cetera, et cetera**."

Coins struck with the likeness of a monarch's head had his title writ around the perimeter, and frequently concluded with the contracted form, **&c.**

Remarkably, linguistic scientists have traced the words **ke-etero, "this remains,"** back to the Indo-European, regarded as the origin of most languages now spoken across Europe and Asia. (One can only imagine hunter-gatherers 10,000 years ago finding it a handy phrase as they tallied and apportioned their nuts, berries and animal skins!) And the need to express the idea of **"and so forth," "and the rest,"** found recognizable words in all the languages that evolved from Indo-European. It resides in Latin languages using some variant of **"et cetera;"** in Dutch **"enzovoort;"** in German **"und so weiter."** It is written in most all languages as an abbreviation: in the above cases, **etc., enz.** and **usw.**

Looking at Hebrew, Hindi and Marathi (a language of western India)... the notion finds expression in some variation of **"ityadi"** meaning **"it is known/sensed."** I find nothing to support this, but I'll bet that our own contemporary **"yadda, yadda, yadda"** is very much a part of the family of expressions that mean **"and so on/you know what I'm saying"** and derives from the same idea as **"ke-etero."** (According to the dictionary, **"Yadda, yadda, yadda"** originated in the 1940s as onomatopoeia, imitating the sound of meaningless chatter.)

We know it was used by Lenny Bruce in the 50s and 60s, but it found its way into current pop culture thanks to the 1997 Seinfeld episode, **"Yada, yada."**) Here's Elaine, "We went out to dinner. I had the lobster bisque. Afterward, we went up to his place, and **yada, yada, yada** ... I never heard from him again." In 2009, the Paley Center awarded it #1 on *TV's 50 Funniest Phrases.*

And so, the expression of an idea once reserved for important people to gloss over information, then used in literature to avoid repeating the obvious, is now employed freely, whimsically, or dismissively, (and often accompanied, when spoken, by the same dramatic gestures that jumped out at me in the Rex Harrison movie). In Tim O'Brien's brilliant 1994 novel, *In The Lake of The Woods,* a former campaign manager says cynically of his candidate, "But John also had ideals. A good progressive Democrat, very dedicated, help the needy, **et cetera, et cetera, ad weirdum**."

"Etceteras," used as a collective noun, has never been admitted to any dictionary, although it has been used informally for at least two hundred years... e.g. "a long list of etceteras," and "the cost of the locomotives and their etceteras ..." It is employed in the same way as "thingamajigs" or "thingamabobs," the latter a popular expression in the 19th century, used by Edgar Allan Poe, and later by Gilbert and Sullivan in *The Mikado.*

One thing is certain, **"etcetera"** in its various iterations will thrive in this complex world where we strain to know all the precise words that proliferate in so many fields, but gloss over them in our communications.

In the La-La Land of Language

EVEN THOUGH:

I've been writing about words for years...
teaching and playing with them too,

I call all kids "abecedarians"
and spread the word "vocabulary,"

I ply the world of etymology
without those pesky flies,

I'm unconfused by tricky English rules,
and know to spell it "jewels" not "jools,"

and "porpoise," I'm sure, is spelt as it is,
and not on "poipose" to confuse
my Brooklyn friends,

I can spell "susurrus" backwards
although it's not a palindrome,

I can unscramble "gsge" and "ocnba" in a sec,
and quickly see the anagram of "speck,"

I learn a new word every day,
like "skosh,"
and look up all the words I've never heard...

"bosky" just yesterday,

I feel the language that's best
uses metaphors for zest,

I do know:
there's still a forever-land before me,
a la-la land of language thrills
as far as I can see.

- Joe Mc Kay
October 2013

Thank you for reading.
Please review this book. Reviews help others find me and inspires me to keep writing!

If you would like to be put on our email list to receive updates on new releases, contests, and promotions, please go to AbsolutelyAmazingEbooks.com and sign up.

About the Author

Joe Mc Kay grew up with a precocious ear for language. Standing in his baby carriage, he "read" aloud the full names of grocery items, e.g., "Kemp's Sun-Rayed Tomato Juice," to audiences of appreciative shoppers as his gloating parents held up the cans and boxes. He listened with wonder to the many accents and dialects he heard in the streets and on the subways and buses of NYC. Contrary to family legend, however, his first words were not *oy vay!*

He studied Latin and French extensively in High School. Later, at Cornell University, his own New York accent yielded to a kind of non-descript Midwestern sound that attendees at his lectures hear today. After graduation he chucked his provincialism altogether as he travelled widely, including living for a time in Germany and Ecuador.

Following a career in labor relations and human resources with Pan American Airways and Avon Products, and as a founding partner of an HR consulting firm, he turned avidly to the study of words, language and literature. "Crazy About Words" was born in 2003.

His ears are ever alert to the sounds of words and to the gestures with which they are delivered, and his eyes are always peeled for how poets and writers use our wonderful English language.

The New
Atlantian Library

NewAtlantianLibrary.com
or AbsolutelyAmazingeBooks.com
or AA-eBooks.com